More **Balanchine** *Variations*

Nancy Goldner

Library of Congress Cataloging-in-Publication Data
Goldner, Nancy.
More Balanchine variations / Nancy Goldner.
p. cm.
Summary: "Provides insightful analysis and description of twenty
Balanchine ballets"— Provided by publisher.
Includes bibliographical references.
ISBN 978-0-8130-3753-0 (pbk.)
1. Balanchine, George. 2. Choreographers—United States.
3. Ballet—History. 4. Choreography—History. I. Title.
GV1785.B32G66 2011
792.82092—dc23
[B]

The University Press of Florida is the scholarly publishing agency
for the State University System of Florida, comprising Florida
A&M University, Florida Atlantic University, Florida Gulf Coast
University, Florida International University, Florida State Uni-
versity, New College of Florida, University of Central Florida,
University of Florida, University of North Florida, University of
South Florida, and University of West Florida.

University Press of Florida
15 Northwest 15th Street
Gainesville, FL 32611-2079
http://www.upf.com

To the memory of my mother, Rose

Contents

Acknowledgments

First and foremost, I am grateful to Meredith Babb, director of the University Press of Florida, for her enduring enthusiasm for this, the second of my Balanchine projects. I extend warmest thanks as well to Barbara Horgan, managing trustee of The George Balanchine Trust, for her votes of confidence over the years; and to Ellen Sorrin, director of the Trust. To the entire staff of the University Press of Florida I owe gratitude for the care they have given to this book. Anna Eberhard Friedlander's knowledge of dance and sensitivity to language made her the ideal copy editor.

Costas supplied the vast majority of photographs for this volume, as he did for the first, and once again I thank him for his diligence, taste, and cheerfulness.

I thank the Corporation of Yaddo in Saratoga Springs, New York, for providing time, space, and quiet—the perfect conditions for writing—and to Peter Kayafas for proposing the idea of going to Yaddo.

For help in sorting out the complexities of the finale to *Symphony in C* I thank Sabrina Pillars, former dancer with the New York City Ballet, and Victoria Simon, also a former member of the company and now a ballet mistress for The George Balanchine Trust.

For each ballet in this volume I worked from a videotape from the archives of the New York City Ballet and The George Balanchine Trust. Thank you to Nicole Cornell, coordinator of the Trust, who with graciousness undertook the task of giving them to me as I needed them. Thanks also to Nancy Reynolds, director of research for The Balanchine Foundation, for providing me with a video of a reconstruction of an early version of *Mozartiana*. Jonathan Vatner gave me valued technical advice, and I am grateful.

The essays on *Mozartiana* and *Episodes* first appeared in the magazine *Dance Now*. I thank this publication for granting me permission to reprint the essays here.

My gratitude to Mary Jane West-Eberhard and Mindy Aloff for their careful reading of the manuscript and their many helpful comments.

Much of the pleasure I took in writing this book I owe to my husband, Jules Cohn, my first and best reader.

Introduction

The twenty ballets discussed in this book begin and end with Tchaikovsky, one of Balanchine's most favored composers. Beyond this happy coincidence, there is no special rhyme or reason to the list, other than the fact that I have already written about another twenty of his ballets in *Balanchine Variations*. The ballets included in that volume were ones I had lectured on across the United States under the auspices of the George Balanchine Foundation. The criteria for selection of the ballets in *More Balanchine Variations* are either that I simply like them—*Raymonda Variations* and *Scotch Symphony*, for example—or that they interest me for particular reasons. *Orpheus* interests me for personal reasons; for one thing, it was the first work that gripped me as a child. *Brahms-Schoenberg Quartet* arouses my curiosity: why doesn't some of it work? Balanchine as a dramatist interests me because not enough attention has been paid to his gifts as a storyteller. Hence *La Valse* and to some extent *Coppélia*. *Symphony in C* and *Liebeslieder Walzer*—why, they're masterpieces. One reason I was eager to write a second volume was to be able to dig into these two works. They're from the top five of the best. *Divertimento No. 15* is certainly from the top ten, plus, it's to Mozart. The Mozart of choreographers, as Balanchine has been called, meets the man himself, on provocative terms.

The chronological range of the ballets in this book is forty years, from 1941 (*Ballet Imperial*, later called *Tschaikovsky Piano Concerto No. 2*) to 1981 (*Mozartiana*, the last complete ballet Balanchine composed before his death two years later). If you include the essays from the first volume, the span in years begins back in 1928, with *Apollo*, his earliest extant ballet. Whether it's forty or fifty-three years of work under consideration, it's natural to want to find an underlying shape, an indication of development, the existence of periods or phases.

There was a change in the way he conceived of ballets. Balanchine worked for Diaghilev and his Ballets Russes from 1924 to 1929, when the impresario died and his company disbanded. The collaborative process by which Diaghilev worked was probably not congenial to Balanchine's sensibilities—that is my intuition—but the importance of scenic designers and librettists in Balanchine's creations extended beyond 1929. Les Ballets 1933, a company formed to present his work in Paris and London, was essentially a Diaghilevian affair. When Balanchine moved to the United States in 1933 at the invitation of Lincoln Kirstein, the Diaghilev spirit traveled across the ocean as well. It was Kirstein who kept the model alive; like Diaghilev, he was a connoisseur of painting and a literary sort of man. He saw the ballet as a vehicle for collaborative aesthetic endeavor, and as an opportunity to commission work from artists he admired. Balanchine's vision of presentation was simpler: classical dancing set to music he liked. I think that the most important development in Balanchine's career was to cast off the influence of other people's visual and literary ideas as the driving force behind ballet. Symbolically, the big change came in 1951, when *Concerto Barocco* and *The Four Temperaments* were shorn of their costumes. From then on, everything you saw on the stage was there exclusively to serve the purpose of the choreographer. This is not to say that decor, costumes, and thematic material had no place on his stage, but it was he who called the shots.

Balanchine idealized women. By temperament he was a romantic, but he was not an optimist. His ballets tell us that he believed love was ephemeral, and this belief was a constant. Coinciding with this streak of fatalism was a down-to-earth practicality. Having worked in so many kinds of situations—on Broadway, in movies, for opera, in nightclubs and in later years for television—he knew how to accommodate the exigencies of commercial theater and different media. He had respect for budgets. If he crossed the line financially (as was the case for *The Nutcracker* or for the Stravinsky Festival of 1972, when the theater shut down for a week), it was artistically necessary. He was not penny-wise, pound foolish, but he did know the value of a dollar. After a rehearsal was over, it was Balanchine who turned off the lights. He was still doing it in 1981.

Except for a period in the 1930s, when he was taken up with gothic-inspired themes, I don't see any phases in Balanchine's work or preoccupations with a particular challenge, but he did go through periods of heightened interest in a dancer. A particularly exciting time was the late 1940s through 1956, because he was creating work for two very different dancers, the virtuoso Maria Tallchief and the dramatically fascinating Tanaquil Le Clercq. For a brief period starting in 1954 Allegra Kent was a muse. Diana Adams captured his imagination beginning in 1957 with *Agon*; for the 1960–61 season Balanchine cast her in no fewer than six works. And then came the Suzanne Farrell era, remarkable for its longevity—from 1963, with *Meditation*, until his death.

Although his love for Farrell damaged the esprit of the rest of the company for several years, overall he took care to keep everyone gainfully employed. Beginning in 1948, when the New York City Ballet was formed, he saw himself as presiding over a family whose contentment was his responsibility. Leafing through programs of his works, you notice the care he took to distribute new roles among his principals each season. Likewise, he had to please the audience. Preempting the "artist" label, he would insist that he was an "entertainer," a "menu planner." A quick scan of the repertory reveals that his self-described epithets were not coy. The predominating characteristic of his repertory was variety—ballets big and small, set to music primarily from the nineteenth and twentieth centuries, with production values ranging from barely anything to extreme opulence.

His earliest extant ballet, *Apollo*, set the artistic bar high. Where could one go from there? In terms of artistic development, his range of subject material and dance style did not so much mature as broaden, depending on his choice of music and the quality of dancers at hand. He had his share of flops and a larger share of masterpieces, and they show up at all points in his career. I don't see any discernible arc in his achievements. One handicap to mapping an arc is that many important ballets are gone: *La Chatte, Errante, Balustrade, The Figure in the Carpet,* and the original versions of *Danses Concertantes* and *Le Baiser de la Fée*. *Cotillon*, another key work, was revived by the Joffrey Ballet in 1988, but that airless production gave little clue to the ballet's much-written-about allure. With them or without, however, it's difficult to locate a peak period; as soon as you think you've found the parameters of the greatest years, along comes a subsequent ballet that skews the theory. As many great works were made in the earlier years as in the later ones. Is there any dance that surpasses the brilliance and range of *Symphony in C*, from 1947? Or the architectural perfection of *Agon*, from 1957? Or the psychological insights of *Liebeslieder Walzer*, from 1960? I think not. Let's say you pick 1960 as the zenith of the curve. Then what do you do with *Jewels* (1967), *Chaconne* (1976), or *Mozartiana* (1981)? I think what you do is separate the Brahms waltz ballet from the rest, because it treats the human heart with a wisdom not found in any other ballet. It's the one ballet I would describe as mature. He was fifty-six years old when he made it, and I can't imagine his having made it at a younger age.

Obviously, a work as intimate and emotionally nuanced as *Liebeslieder* is subject to deterioration when the dancers who worked with Balanchine on it are no longer performing, and when the master himself is no longer around to demonstrate the inflection he wants for each step. In fact, the disparity between how I remember all of the dances discussed in this book and how they look in recent performances recorded on video tape has been the most pervasive challenge in writing about them. Of course, the mere tracking of the choreography on tape reveals Balanchine's intent. His advice to dancers—"just do the steps"—is sound, but it is incomplete. The issue is how richly the steps are done. Showing us the richness involves everything: technical clarity and strength, the ability to listen to the music while dancing, and faith that taking possession of a role can lead one into the center of a particular ballet's world. The hitch is that dancers must first figure out that each ballet does live in its own unique world. Balanchine's ballets are works of art.

These essays are reconstructions based on memory, especially when I write about the choreography's power of expression. They are beholden to the dancers who have taken Balanchine for all he is worth.

Ballet Imperial
(Tschaikovsky Piano Concerto No. 2)

1941

Ballets celebrating the Petipa traditions with which Balanchine grew up in St. Petersburg eventually became the meat and potatoes of his repertory. In 1941, however, when *Ballet Imperial* premiered, he had not yet ventured into Old World territory. Having moved to the United States only recently, in 1933, at the invitation of Lincoln Kirstein, he was probably still intent on staying clear of the nineteenth-century idioms he had left behind. *Ballet Imperial*, set to Tchaikovsky's Piano Concerto No. 2, marked a change of heart. Making a ballet of grandeur to a composer associated with the Russian Imperial age became at this moment commercially and politically expedient.

In 1941 Kirstein was asked by his friend Nelson Rockefeller to prepare a government-subsidized five-month tour of Latin America (Rockefeller was the federal government's Coordinator of Inter-American Affairs, which included cultural affairs). Kirstein naturally asked Balanchine to head up a troupe to be called American Ballet Caravan. For this tour into the unknown, Kirstein and Balanchine agreed that a glamourous Russian-styled ballet would be ideally suited to audiences whom they assumed had conservative tastes, who equated "real" ballet with *Swan Lake* and the like. Of course Balanchine was not inclined to restage nineteenth-century classics, but a modern equivalent would be a shrewd counterweight to the more contemporary ballets to be shown, ballets such as his *Serenade* and the new *Concerto Barocco*.

Thirty-five dancers plus Balanchine and staff set sail on June 6 for Rio de Janeiro, arriving there on June 18. *Ballet Imperial* bowed on opening night, June 25, on a bill that also included *Serenade* and Lew Christensen's *Filling Station*. (*Concerto Barocco*, which turned out to be a masterpiece, premiered two nights later.)

If Balanchine had any resistance to composing a "tutu and tiara" extravaganza, it does not reveal itself in *Ballet Imperial*. I think he had a ball making it. With an ensemble of sixteen women and six men, two female demi-soloists, two male demi-soloists, two female principals, and one cavalier, this was the largest cast for a classical ballet he had ever worked with, and he deployed them with bountiful zest and variety. The cup ran over. Within the first few minutes of the first movement, we see the ensemble in diagonals, diamonds, a huge circle of sixteen women, smaller concentric circles, a pinwheel, and plain old straight lines just for good measure.

Although the technical challenges in other Balanchine ballets tend to be concealed within the choreographic fabric, in *Ballet Imperial* they are boldly, almost gleefully exposed. Or at least they are for the two principal women. Balanchine threw the book at them. He was able to do so because he had in this company two extraordinary virtuosos—Marie-Jeanne and Gisella Caccialanza. Could he have conceived of an imperial ballet without them? I doubt it. But there they were, tossing off all the hardest stuff at allegro tempo—all kinds of pirouettes, jumps, and beats, small, intricate footwork, and moments when they just flew. I think especially of the pas de trois in the first movement, when Caccialanza and two men bound through space in big *jetés* with such force and amplitude so as to banish the perimeters of the stage.

Today, *Ballet Imperial* (or *Tschaikovsky Piano Concerto No. 2*, as it has been known since 1973, with Balanchine's preferred spelling of the composer's name) has achieved legendary status for its virtuosity. The chief hazard for the first ballerina is her first solo, which she dances to one of many piano cadenzas. Several ballerinas are on record about this passage, and they all describe the terror of having to plunge right into the steps without a minute to acclimatize themselves to being on stage, to tell the audience (and themselves), "Here I am." Some speak of the terror of dancing rudderless, without a conductor to supervise the beat. And there is a specific step, repeated five times, that gives the ballerinas heartburn. It's a double pirouette done with the heel of the supporting leg held barely off the ground while the other foot skims along the ground. The idea is to turn without bending the leg and then stop dead, on a dime. If you want more of the gory details, read Merrill Ashley's *Dancing for Balanchine* and a Patricia McBride interview in Nancy Reynolds' *Repertory in Review*.

As for the lady who inspired Balanchine's deviltry, Marie-Jeanne said that the ballet didn't "kill" her, except for that opening cadenza, whereas *Concerto Barocco*, in which she played the first lead, did "kill" her because she was on stage for practically the whole time of seventeen minutes. She did mention doing double *sauts de basques*, a turn in the air that typically is in the man's domain, but that was okay because she liked doing that sort of thing. In the version we see today (there have been several), there are no double *sauts de basques*, nor are there double *tours en l'air*, which Moira Shearer says she did for a production in 1950 with the then Sadler's Wells. Today's dancers can feel that they get off easy.

Ballet Imperial is in three movements. The first is eighteen minutes, half of the entire ballet. Eighteen minutes is a very long time; in fact, it's long enough to be a ballet unto itself, about the same duration as its sibling, *Allegro Brillante*, and *Concerto Barocco*. To keep the juices flowing, Balanchine develops the hierarchical structure of Petipa to an unprecedented degree. In the nineteenth century it was common to set the two principal dancers against an ensemble; those who danced their variations alone were soloists. Only rarely did the three ranks dance together at the same time. It was Balanchine who put them in constant interplay so that different gradations of technical expression could be savored all at once. The full stage picture divided among the many, the few, and the one or two creates its own musical and pictorial drama. And their entrances and exits, multitudinous in *Ballet Imperial*, also provide a gradual layering of excitement. *Ballet Imperial* adds an additional subculture, the demi-soloists. Interestingly, they don't dance by themselves in this ballet; rather, they always accompany the higher-ups. I imagine them as ladies- and men-in-waiting—perhaps fanciful, but given the title of the ballet and the fact that they always maintain a discrete distance behind the principal in the center, I'll stand by my idea.

The big question in the first movement of *Ballet Imperial* is the nature of the hierarchical relationship between the two leading ladies. It matters for the same reason that it matters in literature, because sorting out the question leads you right into the texture and particularities of the book, and engenders an ongoing dialogue between the reader and the writer. In George Eliot's *Daniel Deronda* is it Deronda or Gwendolen Harleth who is most important; in Tolstoy's *War and Peace* is it the Pierre story or the Natasha story that grips us tighter? I'd wager fifty-fifty, and the double-starring nature of these novels makes them all the more fascinating. With the Tchaikovsky ballet, tradition confers first-ballerina status on the one who does the longest cadenza, the one with the treacherous swivel turns, but it is not because of this passage that she comes by that status (the other ballerina has her quota of cadenzas). It's because she does the pas de deux with the cavalier. (The same logic applies to the ranking of the two ballerinas in *Concerto Barocco*.) In Balanchine's ballets, only the pas de deux has the sexual tension and lyrical force that proclaims a woman Number One. Yet the long pas de trois for the so-called second ballerina, who is flanked by two male demi-soloists, is breathtaking enough to hold its own against the pas de deux. When it is danced correctly, with pedal to the metal, the exhilaration of seeing the woman lead the two men in triumphant flight around the stage is supreme. Sometimes it arouses my latent feminist urges. "You go, girl!" I cry silently to the trio. One other thing to notice: Balanchine empties the stage of the ensemble for the trio, giving them limitless space in which to fly. So: who is first and who is second? Of course the pas de deux woman is first, but the fact that you ask the question at all makes the first movement of *Ballet Imperial* unique in the canon.

By the time we move into the second and third parts of the ballet, the question is no longer relevant. If there is one moment, in the final movement, that confers status absolutely, it's yet another new formation of the cast, and one that has never been repeated in other Balanchine ballets. It's when the entire female cast dances on one side of the stage while the first ballerina dances alone on the other side, standing as a counterweight to the group. The balance of weight then shifts as the ensemble joins hands and walks back and forth across the width of the stage, thereby obscuring the ballerina, who gets lost in the shuffle. But then the lines of dancers part to reveal the ballerina alone in stage center, doing that most first-ballerina-ish of turns, the *fouetté*.

In its most literal sense, the most imperial part of *Ballet Imperial* is in the final movement, when the ensemble copies signature phrases from Petipa ballets. (This is the first time since Balanchine's years in the West that he lifted steps from his master, but not the last.) The second movement, an andante, is imperial in its theme. We have here a kind of vision scene, in the spirit of the vision in *The Sleeping Beauty* and the lakeside acts of *Swan Lake*. It features the cavalier and a retinue of ten corps dancers, who trail the man as an amplification of the ladies-in-waiting from the previous section. It begins with the man flanked by five women on each side. To Tchaikovsky's melancholy melody, one wing of women arcs behind the man and runs to the other wing, almost touching the second five dancers with their backs. The tide reverses. The man then runs forward and back, bringing along in his wake a smaller retinue of two women. Then the two women and man run on diagonals, under the arms of the others. Finally, everyone runs together back and forth, back and forth in a swell of choral singing. This might be the most famous moment of *Ballet Imperial* because its poetic urgency is conveyed with daring simplicity. It amazed Mikhail Baryshnikov, who, watching a rehearsal not far from where I was sitting one day, whispered to no one in particular, "It's so simple, so simple," as an incredulous smile beamed his admiration.

The nymphs then form a bower, through which the newly arrived ballerina runs into the arms of the man waiting for her. Tchaikovsky's trembling strings harken to the foreboding of *Swan Lake*, and we know that this love interlude will come to naught. After the couple embrace, the ballerina leaves and the man looks for her among his dream companions,

The ensemble and cavalier in the "vision scene" of *Ballet Imperial*. New York City Ballet. Choreography by George Balanchine © The George Balanchine Trust. Photo © by Costas.

who turn from him with the conventional gesture signifying, "You can't have her." The women then leave, and the man bows to the empty space in memory of his reverie.

There is story enough here, but in the ballet's earlier incarnations, before the title changed to *Tschaikovsky Piano Concerto No. 2*, there was more story. Here is Balanchine, in *Balanchine's Complete Stories of the Great Ballets*: "The ballerina enters with her cavalier. Eight girls form a maze through which the ballerina and her partner move. Now she and her partner are lovers. They appear to be happy, but then the man pleads with her intently and we understand that their love is not perfect. But soon the ballerina responds to her lover's plea and dances with tender intimacy. The corps de ballet dance protectively around the couple and lead them gently into the wings."

The version Balanchine describes is from the original ballet of 1941, and it contained passages of mime. In subsequent years the ballet went through various revisions. In 1950, when Balanchine supervised a production by the Sadler's Wells with Margot Fonteyn, Michael Somes, and Beryl Grey, the pantomime was deleted, there was a new pas de deux in the second movement, and somewhat different groupings in the third. Not until 1964 did the ballet enter the repertory of the New York City Ballet, where it reverted to the first production. Frederic Franklin staged it, having remembered it from the mid-1940s, when the Ballet Russe de Monte Carlo performed it. Finally, in 1973 Balanchine gave it a new production with choreography that, one surmises, followed the Sadler's Wells production. The pantomime was not the only nineteenth-century allusion to get the ax. The title changed to *Piano Concerto No. 2* (and shortly after to *Tschaikovsky Piano Concerto No. 2*). The tutus were out; simple chiffon dresses were in. The original decor, by Mstislav Doboujinsky, placed the dancers on the bank of the Neva River in St. Petersburg. The imperial double eagle hung over the middle of the stage, and in the background

Sofiane Sylve as the first ballerina with Jonathan Stafford as the cavalier in *Ballet Imperial*. New York City Ballet. Choreography by George Balanchine © The George Balanchine Trust. Photo © by Costas.

you could see the Peter and Paul Fortress. This resplendent backdrop was replaced by a plain blue cyclorama—a Balanchine trademark.

Balanchine wanted to modernize the ballet's context because, he said, "There isn't imperial anymore. Only the Empire Hotel," referring to the then run-down hotel across the street from Lincoln Center. To my mind, there is as much imperial in the ballet now as then to warrant its original, and prettier, name. You only have to think of the moment in the first movement when the cavalier escorts the ballerina in front of the corps, who bow to her as she passes. It is revealing to learn of Balanchine's instructions about deportment to the tutu-less ballerina. "Don't look at them! Don't acknowledge them! You're royalty. Royalty doesn't have to bow to anyone. They bow to you and you ignore them," he exhorted Merrill Ashley in 1974.

Of the many ballets prepared for the South American tour, only a few were seen in North America. *Ballet Imperial* and *Concerto Barocco* eventually found a safe berth in the Ballet Russe de Monte Carlo before moving on to other companies. By 1941 the link between Balanchine and the Ballet Russe was strong. It was already dancing *Serenade*, *Le Baiser de la Fée*, and *Card Game*. By mid-1944 the company was free to offer, and Balanchine was free to accept, the post of resident choreographer. In September of that year his new *Danses Concertantes*, to the Stravinsky score of the same name, was up and running. *Ballet Imperial* and *Concerto Barocco* also entered the repertory now, as well as a reworking of *Mozartiana*, from 1933.

Between 1944 and 1946 the Ballet Russe could justifiably be called a Balanchine company. In addition to the Stravinsky ballet he created four others during these years: *Night Shadow* (later called *La Sonnambula*), a new version of *Le Bourgeois Gentilhomme*, a pas de deux to music from *The Sleeping Beauty* for the company's stars, Alexandra Danilova and Frederic Franklin (whom Balanchine appointed ballet master), and an abbreviated version of the full-length *Raymonda*. It was a Balanchine company in another important way as well. Often teaching company class, including when the troupe was on tour, he is thought to have transformed the dancers' old-fashioned technique and dance style into the unmannered, precise ensemble that would eventually become synonymous with the so-called Balanchine style.

I was not yet a dance-goer in the Ballet Russe years, and I am always impressed by, if not a little jealous of, the beautiful memories dance fans have of those years. Among them was the critic Edwin Denby, who cut his teeth on the Ballet Russe repertory and the dancing of Danilova, Maria Tallchief, Mary Ellen Moylan, Patricia Wilde, Franklin, and Marie-Jeanne. Who knows for how long the association might have lasted had not Kirstein, returned from the war, drawn up a plan called Ballet Society, which was designed to give Balanchine the artistic and financial independence he had not secured since moving to the United States. So in 1946 Balanchine left the Ballet Russe de Monte Carlo to create a new repertory for Ballet Society. The plan worked out well. One of the new works was *Orpheus*, which led to Ballet Society becoming the New York City Ballet in 1948.

Symphony in C

1947

Balanchine was a master of the finale, and the finale of *Symphony in C* was his masterpiece. With an enormous cast of fifty-two, it was destined to be a winner, but what gives it the blue ribbon is one iconic moment: when the thirty-six women of the ensemble ring the perimeters of the stage and do a series of simple leg and arm movements, while the four principal women pirouette madly in stage center. While the strings of the Bizet score are whirring equally madly, Balanchine gives us a panoramic view of controlled, organized activity. It's like looking into a beehive, except that Balanchine's bees wear white tutus.

It's fun to subject such a supreme moment to the what-if game. What if the ensemble were not grouped into pristine lines? Well, there's nothing as powerful as a line; you need only think of the procession of the shades in the dream scene of *La Bayadère*, or of the Rockettes in their *grand battement* routine. What if the corps and principals were dancing in unison? Well, that's always exciting, but what we do see—a contrast between the more simple steps of the ensemble and the intensity of the principals' pirouettes—is in exciting counterpoint to the music, which at the moment is "dancing" in unison. And then there's the matter of playing one's hand judiciously in what is the fourth movement's long finale. There will be unison dancing, but it will come later, toward the very end of the ballet.

As perfect as the setup is, however, it doesn't quite explain the brilliance of the moment. What if the ensemble did a simple series of *tendus* and corresponding arm movements? It would be splendid—with so many legs and arms moving, it couldn't be anything less—but Balanchine adds a few complications that give the visual and kinetic fabric of the choreography even more texture. The legs move front and side in *tendu* rather than in one direction, but they don't move absolutely front and side. That might end up being flat and heavy. Balanchine shades the direction by having the dancers stand at an angle to the audience. Thus, the foot moves forward in a *croisé*, or crossed, position and to the side in *écarté*, or on a diagonal. The arms, meanwhile, change every time the dancers switch from *croisé* to *écarté* and back again. Taking in the whole stage picture with one gulp, you notice (or eventually notice) that while the principals are galloping ahead in four beats to the measure, the ensemble is moving in three beats. Thus, the new dance measure for the ensemble begins just before the principals' next measure.

The *tendus* have their own complications. After much squinting at a videotape with the help of Sabrina Pillars, a former dancer with the New York City Ballet, and Victoria Simon, a ballet mistress for The George Balanchine Trust, I hereby present the recipe for those *tendus*. On count one the right foot moves forward. On count two it moves to the side and closes in fifth position behind the standing leg. On count three the leg moves to the side again, and closes in fifth position with the moving leg in front. This set is done two times on the same working leg. On the third set, however, the dancers do only two *tendus*, front and side. The dancers on the left side of the stage close front, and those on the right side close back, so that each side is a mirror image of the other. They do three more sets like the first two, except that the working leg changes each time and each side has the opposite working leg. At this point the ensemble stops dead in its tracks while the principals keep the momentum going by fairly pounding the floor with *bourrées*.

The moral is that there's more to the *tendu* story than meets the eye. Its pattern is asymmetrical, and its counts for the ensemble don't jibe with those for the principals. Finally, although the whole *tendu* section

The Bolshoi Ballet in *Symphony in C*. Choreography by George Balanchine
© The School of American Ballet. Photo © by Costas.

looks like unison dancing, only the first half truly is. It doesn't matter all that much whether you catch the irregularities right away, upon repeated viewings, or not at all. They are felt subliminally. Sensing them is sufficient to make the whole passage vibrant and light and unpredictable.

Of course, even at its most superficial level the mere sight of all those legs and arms moving together (more or less) makes the spirit soar no matter how many times you see the ballet. And the spectacle is always something of a surprise—despite the fact that Balanchine has been dropping clues along the way. The first thing the eight corps women do in the first movement is a sequence of *tendus*. In the fourth, last movement the women line up and *tendu* in counterpoint to the principal couple's more

intricate steps. And the table is all but laid out before our eyes in the prelude to the big moment. This prelude—the second half of the fourth movement—is a recapitulation of the first three. Each of the casts rushes on and repeats (with some variation) signature moments of its choreography. At the end of their respective encores the principals exit, while the ensemble steps to the sides of the stage and poses. Slowly the perimeters of the stage fill in, so that by the time the principal women return to begin their pirouettes, the entire ensemble is assembled and ready to go.

This *tendu* extravaganza takes less than a minute, and there is much more finale derring-do to come. In typical Balanchine fashion, the excitement simmers down and then builds again as the four ballerinas enter and repeat their turns and then join all the women in a jamboree of dancing. Just as the clock strikes midnight, all fifty-two dancers form a fabulous tableau: the corps poses on its toes, the eight female demi-soloists are lifted onto their partners' shoulders, and the ballerinas stand in *passé* and snap their torsos way, way over to the side. All of this contrasting movement happens in a flash, and the curtain drops. The audience feels that it has been splashing in the fountain of youth.

George Bizet was all of seventeen years old when he wrote *Symphony in C* in 1855. The score gathered dust for many years in the Conservatoire de Paris. Some musicologists believe that Bizet kept it hidden away because he felt it was too derivative. Not until 1935 was the symphony given a public performance. The wording in the New York City Ballet's program note for *Symphony in C* suggests that Balanchine was the first to choreograph to the score. This is not so. First honors goes to Andrée Howard. She set the music on the junior company of the Sadler's Wells, in London, where it premiered in April 1946 under the name *Assembly Ball*. Balanchine heard about the score not from London sources, but from Stravinsky. When he traveled to Paris in February 1947 to begin a six-month residency as ballet master at the opera house, he chose this French music as the vehicle for a new ballet for the Paris Opera. It premiered on July 28, 1947, under the name *Le Palais de Cristal*, reflecting the sumptuous decor and costumes by Leonor Fini. The tunics and tutus were in a different color for each of the four movements. When the ballet premiered in New York on March 22, 1948, as part of a Ballet Society bill, the crystal palace was replaced by a simple blue cyclorama; the tutus were all white and the men's tunics black.

Bizet composed his first symphony in five weeks. Balanchine choreographed to it in two. The speed with which Balanchine worked was typical. Whether Bizet was as nimble I do not know, but certainly both compositions have an exuberance and spontaneity suggesting that the Muse sat very near as both artists worked. As for the ballet, every step, every pattern, and every compositional device flows so naturally and effortlessly out of the music that the choreography hardly seems a translation from one medium into another. Undoubtedly the ballet underwent some translation as it crossed the ocean from Paris to New York, particularly if it enhanced the special talents of the dancers. Maria Tallchief, the lead in the first movement in New York, thinks that Balanchine added some pirouettes for her; she was a champion turner. My hunch is that in the adagio movement in Paris, Tamara Toumanova had a few more balances than her American counterpart, Tanaquil Le Clercq. I surmise this because Balanchine often told the story of how he gave Toumanova lots of balances because it was a specialty of hers. But what happened at the premiere? The great balancer kept falling off pointe. He told this story as a warning to young dancers rehearsing difficult pas de deux. Don't stop when you make a flub; flubs are inevitable, he would say. The point of rehearsals was to prepare for "disaster," as he called it.

I am not sure that Balanchine actually did alter the adagio to ward off disaster—or, indeed, that he significantly altered it at all. It so happens that there was a perfect opportunity to compare versions when in 1986 the Paris Opera Ballet performed *Le Palais de Cristal* at the Metropolitan Opera in New York. But the opportunity eluded me because I was so disoriented by the different-colored tutus that I could not focus on what the dancers were doing. The American *Symphony in C* nails the music so perfectly that it seems impossible, my ignorance notwithstanding, to imagine Balanchine doing it any other way.

Sometimes Balanchine captures the music with unusual literalness, especially in the third movement. When the main musical theme repeats itself, so does the choreography for the lead couple—step for step, from their brilliant leaps around the stage to the ballerina's fast pirouettes ending in a faster dip into an arabesque *penchée*. Balanchine cheerfully follows the music's command with no ifs, ands, or buts. My favorite example of this, also in the third movement, is when the violins are in a brief holding pattern before the main theme takes over. The dancers mimic the music's anticipatory feeling by quickly springing up onto pointe and down four times. Yes, Balanchine is Mickey-Mousing the music, but to wander from Bizet's irresistible beat would be perverse.

Mostly Balanchine captures the music's spirit with parallel constructs. Except for the second, adagio movement, the score is allegro. It contrasts bold, declarative statements, especially in the first, most developed movement, with melodies that sing; indeed, you can't help but sing them to yourself. The dancing, likewise, alternates between fast, emphatic footwork and broader, spacious movement. This dualism is seen right off the bat with the ensemble and two demi-soloist couples. The first motif is a little curtsy to the front leg, then a sharp hop onto pointe, then a fast, even sharper twist of the whole torso so that the dancers face to the back. That's a lot of robust dancing packed into three beats. Soon they take large steps sideways, ending with their bodies softly stretched sideways, picking up the music's singing quality. In some of the loveliest moments of the first movement the ensemble, split into two groups, volleys a phrase back and forth, which makes you hear the music's dialogue between the bold and the delicate.

This contrast is seen most concretely in the choreography for the ballerina in the first movement—in her elongated arabesques and loping canters with her partner versus the delicate but strong thrusts of her pointes into the floor. There are few roles that challenge the dancer to move so rapidly between almost percussive vigor and largesse. To my mind, the principal in the first movement is the ballet's heroine. But she is an unsung heroine, for two reasons. First, the ensemble fairly dominates the stage, so rich and ever-present is its dancing. Second, it's the adagio woman who has the glamour, as always.

The adagio ballerina in *Symphony in C* is perhaps the most prized role in the Balanchine repertory. To contemporary dancers she is what Odette used to signify to ballerinas of earlier generations. This Bizet ballerina is imperturbable. She moves in one long, sustained pulse unbroken by breathing (so it seems). Aided by her cavalier, she glides through the air without ever touching ground (so it seems). Balanchine likened her to "the moon gliding across the sky." Yet she does not dwell alone in her own universe. Following the example of the adagio in *Concerto Barocco*, Balanchine sets the dancers in interplay right from the beginning. As a prelude to the entrance of the ballerina and her partner, the demi-soloist couples make a bridge over the ensemble, who nod as the two couples walk by. As the ballerina does big arabesques soon after, the demi-soloists enclose her and her cavalier with their arms. And when she's lifted across the stage in an arabesque, her partner dips her into the middle of a circle the demi-soloists make with their arms, as if they were awaiting her arrival. You might say that these courtesies are recognition of rank, but they

Suzanne Farrell and Peter Martins near the end of the *Symphony in C* adagio, observed by dancers in the wings. New York City Ballet. Choreography by George Balanchine © The School of American Ballet. Photo © by Costas.

also bespeak tenderness, care, and intimacy—all the qualities we might wish for in our own communities.

In the *Barocco* adagio these niceties are continuous. In this adagio, however, they function as preliminaries for the main musical event, which is the introduction of Bizet's second theme for this movement. The six women of the ensemble *bourrée* toward the back of the stage under the arms of the demi-soloists. The men exit and the women recede to the back and sides, clearing the space for the ballerina and cavalier, who leads her forward. As the grand melody begins, she slowly lifts her leg in a *grand développé à la seconde*, a moment, which, as followers of Petipa's and Balanchine's ballets know, creates a special gravity, the coronation, if you will, of the ballerina. In the following passages—of difficult balances, hushed lifts, and deep arabesques *penchées*—she does indeed seem to exist in her own universe. Then the spell is broken with a fugue. The ensemble joins the ballerina again with the sharp movements befitting a fugue. The return of the oboe theme, which began the adagio, heralds the return of the ballerina as the gliding moon. At the end, her partner drapes her over his knee and slowly rotates her in a circle as she sinks closer and closer to the floor. As she is reaching her final resting place, the demi-soloists make a bridge over the ensemble and pass by in arabesques; the ensemble responds by lunging forward. Whereupon the audience takes its first breath in some nine minutes.

There was one occasion when the audience was literally breathless. On January 16, 1976, Suzanne Farrell marked her homecoming to the City Ballet in this adagio, after an absence of six years. Balanchine sets the stage for the ballerina's entrance with a relatively long introduction by the ensemble and demi-soloists. I don't think I've ever felt such stillness in the audience during this prelude; in retrospect I sometimes ask myself, What were we expecting? Was it the mere sight of Farrell after so many years that had us all on edge? When at long, long last, it seemed, she slowly *bourréed* onstage, her face was so rapt and her body so attuned to the sad strains of the oboe that you felt the years of her hiatus evaporate. She was paler and thinner than you remembered, but she was the artist she had always been.

Symphony in C has been the occasion for countless other debuts, though unheralded. By company tradition, City Ballet apprentices step onto the stage for the first time with the company in the fourth movement. I often think of the exhilaration these novices must feel when they participate in the festival of *tendus*. Something of that exhilaration could be felt when Mikhail Baryshnikov danced the lead in the third movement in 1978. He obviously had a great time soaring in circles around the stage, but it was in the finale that he seemed most happy. For once, he was a player in a grand show rather than the show himself. He looked more at home in *Symphony in C* than in any other ballet he performed during his year and a half with the City Ballet.

Symphony in C makes everyone happy—and more. Watching it is a rejuvenating experience. Since its New York premiere in March 1948 it has joined works like *Serenade*, *The Four Temperaments*, *Concerto Barocco*, and *Agon* as definitions of classical ballet at the City Ballet. But I don't think that any of them lifts the spirit in such an irresistibly straightforward way as the Bizet.

Orpheus

1948

In terms of institutional history, *Orpheus* is the most important ballet ever to be produced by Balanchine and Kirstein, because it led in 1948 to the transformation of the struggling Ballet Society into an organization that would be subsidized, the New York City Ballet.

Founded in 1946, Ballet Society had no home, and so for its upcoming program in March 1948 Kirstein rented New York's City Center. Having fallen on hard times during the Depression, this theater had been taken over by the city, which under the innovative leadership of Mayor Fiorello La Guardia had used it for cultural attractions with reasonable ticket prices. One day Morton Baum, the chief financial executive of the theater, wandered into rehearsals for *Symphony in C* and *Orpheus*. According to Baum, he had an epiphany upon seeing *Orpheus*, overwhelmed by the beauty of what he saw. (I'm surprised that Baum was not equally impressed with the Bizet ballet, but considering the results of his epiphany, one must not quibble.) The next day an exuberant Baum visited Kirstein, whom he had never met, but was taken aback by Kirstein's doomsday mood. It was not until shortly after the premiere of *Orpheus*, on April 28, that Baum formally invited Ballet Society to become a resident of the City Center, joining the New York City Opera. One condition was that the ballet had to be responsible for its deficit. Thanks to a check from his mother, by mid-September Kirstein had lowered the deficit enough to feel free to accept Baum's offer. On October 11, 1948, the New York City Ballet made its debut with a blockbuster bill—*Orpheus, Symphony in C,* and *Concerto Barocco*—and the company was off and running.

Not so *Orpheus*. Today the ballet is in limbo, neither lost nor found. It was revived in 1972 for the Stravinsky Festival, with Isamu Noguchi's scenery enlarged to fill out the stage of the New York State Theater, which is much larger than the City Center's. Since then it has been performed sporadically, sometimes for state occasions, such as the tenth anniversary of Balanchine's death, sometimes to honor a special dancer, such as Baryshnikov or Nureyev. The best clue as to what the first *Orpheus* might have looked like is in a video (filmed for the Balanchine Foundation's Interpreters Archive) of Maria Tallchief, the original Eurydice, coaching another dancer in her short Hades solo. In this solo, Eurydice pleads for her release from death, and what's particularly lovely about Tallchief's dancing is the way she alternates between resignation and yearning.

At its premiere *Orpheus* was critically acclaimed, although not universally. Among the naysayers was the critic Robert Garis, for whom the highlight of the evening was going to the Sixth Avenue Delicatessen after the performance and seeing Balanchine and Tallchief there. The ballet was also a box-office hit. No doubt its commissioned score by Stravinsky, who conducted the first performance, endowed the ballet with prestige, but it's difficult to imagine the ballet being even a temporary cash cow. Today it would be impossible for the audience to know what the fuss was about on any terms. It's hard to know what *Orpheus* is about, period. It is in a different language from the one dancers and the public know. Stravinsky wrote, "I visualized the character of this music as a long, sustained slow chant. . . ." Balanchine embodied this depiction perfectly in his choreography, which is why the ballet is out of one's reach today. Orpheus moves with muted gesture and breath, as do his friends, who come to comfort him, and the Dark Angel, who leads him into Hades. Orpheus especially is soft with sorrow. Eurydice, in her solo in Hades, gathers her energy but then sinks back into herself. There is relatively little dancing in *Orpheus*, and what dancing there is is subsumed by an overarching meditative pace. Likewise the music. In the dance of the furies and later on of the bacchantes, you hear the Stravinskyan syncopations and percussive throbs,

Karin von Aroldingen in *Orpheus*. New York City Ballet. Choreography by
George Balanchine © The George Balanchine Trust. By permission of New York
City Ballet, Media and Domestic Rights Owner. Photo © by Costas.

but when the music is over what lingers most is the plaintive plucking of
the harp (representing the lyre). Audiences today expect not gesture but
"real" dancing, with the dancers' bodies held high and proud and taut.
The style of *Orpheus* goes against the grain of the dancers' training as well.
When I was a student at the School of American Ballet, the worst thing
the teacher could say was that you moved like spaghetti. Orpheus moves
like spaghetti. His most typical posture is concave.

Yet the ballet is one of the most perfectly thought-out ballets Balanchine ever made, in which choreography, music, decor, and lighting
play equally important roles. Noguchi ventured to say that *Orpheus* is the
"story of an artist blinded by his vision (the mask)." So, too, is the audience blinded, blinded by the murky darkness in which Jean Rosenthal,
the original lighting designer, embedded much of the action. One of the
most potent aspects about the production is negative—once Orpheus

reaches Hades, you can barely make out the dancers. As I remember it, the perimeters of the stage seemed nonexistent. Characters emerged and receded, but from where? The darkness had no boundaries. On earth, where the light was brighter, scorchingly so in the scene where the bacchantes kill Orpheus, the atmosphere was thin. In Hades, it was thick with shadows and half-perceived images. Another Rosenthal touch is the famous silk curtain that drops when Orpheus and the angel embark on their journey to the underworld and drops again when Orpheus and Eurydice begin their climb toward home. The curtain was not Rosenthal's idea; it was inspired by a curtain Pavel Tchelitchev used for an earlier Balanchine ballet, *Errante*. But under Rosenthal's guidance, the curtain didn't merely drop. It floated, billowed, had a life of its own. When Eurydice dies, the curtain became a living tomb into which she was sucked by shadowy figures and the currents of the silk itself, stirred to move by unseen forces. In thinking about the ballet when it was first done, one is tempted to call Rosenthal the prime mover.

Noguchi's costumes and decor are too explicitly sexual for my taste; indeed, a spectator in an impish frame of mind might find comical all those horns and spiky protuberances jutting out from the wings. Their sharp outlines contradict the lament of the music and dancing. But Noguchi's idea of having the Dark Angel wrapped in a long rope gave Balanchine a visual metaphor with which he could enwrap the entire ballet. When the Dark Angel first enters, he "bonds" with Orpheus by slithering out of his coil and winding it around Orpheus's arms. The lyre itself becomes an object of connectedness, for the angel and Orpheus clasp their hands through the lyre's opening as they travel to Hades. Orpheus has two pas de deux, one for the two men, when the angel helps persuade a reticent (perhaps exhausted) Orpheus to pluck the lyre in order to calm the furies and persuade Pluto to yield Eurydice to the two supplicants. The other, longer duet is danced by husband and wife on their journey back from Hades. Both duets are built around two bodies intertwining. The Orpheus/Eurydice one is incredibly inventive for the many ways she snakes her body around her beloved; you could call the duet acrobatic were it not for the fact that you are as engaged with what her spectacular maneuvers express: her longing for him and his resistance.

Amar Ramasar as the Dark Angel and Ask la Cour as Orpheus. New York City Ballet. Choreography by George Balanchine © The George Balanchine Trust. By permission of New York City Ballet, Media and Domestic Rights Owner. Photo © by Costas.

It was unusual for Balanchine to use explicitly metaphorical movement as pervasively as he did in *Orpheus*. Perhaps it was the telling of the story, rather than choreography, that was uppermost in his mind. (In the dance of the furies, choreographic ideas pretty much failed him, for it is a silly dance. Sometimes I imagine Balanchine rethinking the ballet and cutting the furies population out of the story entirely.) With the exception of the furies dance, nothing in *Orpheus* is superfluous, and the dramatic motivation that supports the choreography combines with all the other elements of the production to make the ballet more "unified," to use a favorite critical value, than any other Balanchine ballet I can think of.

As a child I was drawn to Balanchine for the same reason everyone else was and is: there is so much beautiful, exciting dancing. There is so much to see! In *Orpheus* there is so much that cannot be seen. Perhaps this is one reason why it was *Orpheus*, and not *The Firebird* or *Serenade* or any of the other marvelous ballets I saw when I was six or seven years old, that really hooked me. It was my favorite ballet. The darkness, the silk curtain, the rocks floating upward as Orpheus heads downward, the tendrils of music accompanying the lyre as it ascends heavenward in the apotheosis—whose sound reminded Balanchine of the river along which Orpheus's head floats in Ovid's telling of the myth—all of it gripped me in its mysteriousness. And of course there was the story itself. The seven-year-old's mind wanted to know why: Why did he look back? Why did she have to die? Why couldn't they have at least one more pas de deux before she disappeared behind the curtain? I demanded from my mother answers, each of which I argued against with all my logical force but to no avail, because none of my replies could answer her final reason: Eurydice dies because that is the way the story goes.

It's a very good story. It was on Balanchine's mind long before he made *Orpheus*, when in 1936 he produced for the Metropolitan Opera Gluck's *Orpheus and Eurydice*. Perhaps it was still on his mind in 1976, when he staged the Gluck music again for the New York City Ballet in *Chaconne*. I for one like to think that in *Chaconne*'s opening pas de deux, set to Gluck's depiction of the Elysian Fields, Balanchine gives the lovers the happy ending denied them in Stravinsky's *Orpheus*. In my own life, too, the story returned in another form. As my mother lay fairly unconscious following a stroke, I used to sing to her, hoping to rouse her from her semi-death so that she would grant me just one glance of recognition. Change the story, I would say to my mother. But she didn't. It's the story.

When Balanchine and Stravinsky began to work on *Orpheus* in 1946, it was the story that guided them in figuring out the music's shape. Balanchine's description of the process, given in an interview with Jonathan Cott, is typically offhand, yet informative. "I would visit Stravinsky's home in California and we'd talk. 'What do you want to do?' he'd ask, and I'd say, 'Supposing we do *Orpheus*.' 'How do you think *Orpheus* should be done?' 'Well,' I'd say, 'a little bit like an opera. . . . ' 'Now, where to begin?' And I said, 'Eurydice is in the ground, she's already buried, Orpheus is sad and cries—friends come to visit him, and then he sings and plays.' 'Well,' Stravinsky asked, 'how long does he play? . . . How long would you like him to stand without dancing, without moving? A sad person stands for a while, you know.' 'Well,' I said, 'maybe at least a minute.' So he wrote down 'minute.' 'And then,' I said, 'his friends come in and bring something and leave.' 'How long?' asked Stravinsky. I calculated it by walking. 'That will take about two minutes.' He wrote it down. And it went on like that."

The scenario was finished at Stravinsky's home over a two-day period in April 1946. By the fall of 1947 Stravinsky had orchestrated it, mailing it section by section to Balanchine in New York. Balanchine began choreographing it in early 1948. Stravinsky attended rehearsals and reworked passages of the score to accommodate Balanchine's needs. One time, Stravinsky asked Tallchief how much time she needed to die. She rested her head on the shoulder of Nicholas Magallanes, who played Orpheus, and slipped to the floor. Stravinsky snapped his fingers four times; good, he said, you die in four beats. He marked that measure with silence. According to Charles Joseph, in *Stravinsky & Balanchine: A Journey of Invention*, the silence necessitated a good deal of revision of the score, but it's a wonderful theatrical moment if you catch it.

Stravinsky wrote that in devising the scenario he and Balanchine used Ovid's version of the myth. They did not include the part where Orpheus's head floats down a river, and they added their personal interpretation of the story in an apotheosis. In the final scene, Apollo appears with the mask worn by Orpheus, now greatly enlarged. He raises the mask to the skies and cradles it in his arms; Orpheus, after all, is the son of Apollo. Apollo then walks to the mound where Orpheus was killed, and summons the lyre to rise out of the ground and float slowly upward into, one gathers, eternal time. At a dress rehearsal of *Orpheus* for the 1972 Stravinsky Festival, I was able to watch Balanchine move with the mask as he coached the dancer playing Apollo. He handled the mask as if it were both a holy relic and a personal memento: thus Apollo as god and father. His body was always moving—grandly, tenderly, and slowly. He looked comfortable moving slowly; he was not afraid of stillness. The dancer he was instructing followed him breath by breath, but he could not grasp the stillness. And he wanted to embellish the movements Balanchine did, as if not trusting that the symbolic power of the mask made anything but the simplest movement superfluous.

La Valse

1951

Balanchine said that he owed half of the success of his ballets to Karinska, the costume designer whose exquisite tutus embodied the Russian, Fabergé side of him. In *La Valse*, Karinska's dresses are not only the medium but the message. The ballet glorifies glamour, and Karinska expressed the idea in her long tulle gowns of infinite coloration. The ballet is mysterious, and so are the costumes. On the surface they appear to be basically of one color, but when the dancers lift the outer layers of tulle a ravishing panoply of color is revealed—oranges, crimsons, pinks, blues, lavenders. Depending on the extent to which the dancers revel in the display of their attire, you could say that the love they have for it ranges from much to too much. It's the latter that points to the ballet's theme.

The origin of these dresses can be traced to Balanchine's *Cotillon*, a now mostly lost ballet made in Europe in 1932 for the Ballet Russe de Monte Carlo. Christian Bérard was the designer and Karinska the translator of his concept into actuality. In 1949, for *Bourrée Fantasque*, Balanchine asked Karinska to design as well as execute. *La Valse*, which premiered in 1951, was the second ballet she designed. Keeping the basic idea of the luxuriously layered dresses for the women of *Cotillon*, she modernized their cut by reducing the material around the hips and constructing very tight halter-style bodices in steel gray. The line was slimmer and longer, paralleling the physical change of Balanchine's dancers from the 1930s in Europe to America in the 1950s. Many say that Karinska's costumes for *La Valse* also reflected the haute couture of the time, but to my eyes Dior can't hold a candle to the chic of *La Valse*.

La Valse is set to Ravel's Valses Nobles et Sentimentales, composed of eight waltzes, plus his La Valse. Ravel's epigram for the latter—"We are dancing on the edge of a volcano"—Balanchine translates into a morality tale about a society that prizes elegance too much. He lays out the story in the second waltz (the first is used as an overture), veers around it in later waltzes, gives a few false leads, and then picks up the scent again in the eighth waltz and through La Valse. Although he keeps us guessing about the story's outcome, the imagery he uses is constant. Thus we sense what is coming but don't know how it will reveal itself. In *La Valse* Balanchine has composed an elegantly crafted fable for our time.

Set ironically against Karinska's idealization of the Romantic tutu, the choreography distorts the idea of beauty and elegance with eccentric, overly stylized arm movement. It's all encapsulated in the second waltz. The curtain rises on three women standing in a line. One of their arms rests against the forehead, and the other is placed just below the hip. The placement of their arms, languorous and seductive, is accentuated by long, long white gloves. The figure their bodies cut is sharp—all elbows and wrists. As the dance progresses, their arms take on increasing contrivance. They bend their elbows into the sides of their torsos, so that their arms look like chicken wings. (The chicken-wing image Balanchine has used to humorous effect in other ballets, such as *Rubies*, but here it is bizarre.) They flatten their forearms against each other, while their hands cup their faces. This unnaturalness is alluring precisely because it is so unnatural; it also makes you wince. With their elbows lifted high and outward, they rotate their hands as if talking to each other in signs. In one of the most fabled ports de bras, the ladies lift one arm straight up while the other is crossed; the critic Arlene Croce has written of them as "crosses in a graveyard." The metaphorical richness of this short dance has set other imaginations on fire. Here is the historian Richard Buckle on the dance, in *Balanchine: Ballet Master*: " . . . holding up their arms affectedly in a way that appears to proclaim their charming but sinister authority.

The three fates of *La Valse*: Ellen Bar, Deanna McBrearty, and Saskia Beskow (*left to right*). New York City Ballet. Choreography by George Balanchine © The George Balanchine Trust. Photo © by Costas.

They are society's witches, who console themselves for the loss of youth by the exercise of power. As they dance, their hands make absurd, coy, mannered gestures, which seem traditional signs, like the language of an eighteenth-century fan."

But who actually are they? As sometimes happens, Balanchine retreats from his theme for a while with lighter and more spacious waltzes. It's not until the trio reappears, in ominous lighting, that you feel the significance of their threesomeness. Their identity as the three fates gains further credence when they cross their arms over a lone man's face, blinding him. They whirl around him and rush at him with big jumps, drawing him into their dance. Then the women leave. Couples now run across the stage at seemingly random intervals, their arms and dresses swirling. The man's arms swirl with them. Once again, the threesome appears. They encircle the man and all run off. Riddles are also swirling. Does the man invoke the heady dreams he is having, or is he a victim of them? Is he the hero of the ballet? Or is it the three fates around whom the story will play out?

In the eighth, final waltz a woman in white enters the arena. The color of her dress singles her out, of course, but so do the psychological nuances of her dancing. As she makes her way across the stage, she thrusts her arms and body forward, then pulls back. She both seeks and rejects. She is both strong and fragile, for when she pulls her elbows sharply into her waist, she is like an oyster shivering from the impact of drops from a lemon. (This creature does not live in nature; her domain is on the half-shell.)

A man we have not seen before appears, and he and the woman in white exchange a dialogue of gestures that is both elaborately detailed yet arcane. Their conversation is all form and no content. Several times she retreats to a corner, only to succumb to a magnetic force that unites them again. With studied timing, they repeat their exquisite dialogue of arms and hands; you notice the flexibility of her wrists, the ornate configurations of her arms, the way her elbows pierce the black space around her. As she briefly rests her head on her partner's shoulders, as if to seek respite from her contrived gestures, a deathly mask-like face emerges from the shadows, and his face follows the couple as she is lifted in restless semicircles into the wings.

The orchestra rumbles the opening bars of La Valse. The three fates suddenly present themselves in the hot glare of a spotlight, then disappear. Others rush across the stage, finding their partners or not. All is in flux, fragmentation. But slowly the pieces coalesce into a coherent line of ladies and gentlemen, and a formal waltz begins. More and more dancers fill the ballroom in legible formations; at one point, a woman leads an ensemble of eight waltzers here arranged in two neat rows. Their feet move quickly in *jetés battus, emboîtés*, and other small jumps. We understand the language; it's classical ballet. But when the woman in white and her partner swirl on, all language stops. They are engulfed in the drive of the waltz, until the figure of death enters once more. Suddenly the dancers sink to the floor, and the partner of the woman in white freezes. Now Death and the beautiful lady reenact the dance she did with her partner in the previous section. She resists Death's call at first, then succumbs. He presents her with gifts—a black necklace, black gloves into which she plunges her arms, a black dress that she dons over her white dress, and finally a bouquet of black flowers. She is horrified by her appearance when

Death gives her a cracked mirror with which to admire the necklace, and she throws her bouquet to the floor in disgust. But she is, in Martha Graham's phrase, "doom eager."

Francisco Moncion, who played Death through the 1970s, describes his victim, originally Tanaquil Le Clercq, this way in Nancy Reynolds' *Repertory in Review*: "The quality Tanny gave to the character was a kind of discontent and then an avidity—not really greed—for reaching out to something new. . . . Somehow, with the Death figure, it's the allure of the unknown that tantalizes her. She clutches the necklace, tries it on, and suddenly something fulfilling begins to happen. . . ." Death waltzes her in circles faster and faster. He clasps her body to his, and then all but throws her body to the floor before running off the stage.

The violence of his gesture shatters the ballet's veneer of elegant manners. Balanchine breaks the shell again when the partner of the dead girl literally drags the corpse to the back of the stage. The audience sees this, but the dancers don't. They resume their dancing, and when the music reaches a climax, they dance in unison. It's a grand spectacle, this finale, but it's not the final finale. The corpse is carried to stage center where she is held aloft, pitching and heaving in the hands of her pallbearers, while the rest run in circles around her. Outside of the swarm stands her partner, swaying his arms in time to the music, whether in farewell or in the thrall of the waltz we do not know.

I've gone into detail about *La Valse*'s story because, as always, it's in the details that you appreciate the care with which Balanchine has staged his *Liebestod*. He builds to the climax with precision, so that when it arrives it seems inevitable yet no less shocking.

"Sinister" is the word Cecil Beaton used to describe an undercurrent of *Cotillon*, the ballet that was the inspiration for *La Valse*'s costumes. Beaton attributed that quality to the color of the costumes, while others have found a touch of the sinister in some of the events that happen in the ballet, especially the Hand of Fate duet. Other Balanchine ballets made in the same period as *Cotillon*, in the early 1930s, are also possible ancestors of *La Valse*: *The Seven Deadly Sins*, *Les Songes*, *Errante*, and *Transcendance*. I am on thin ice here, because these ballets are no longer extant, but their librettos and the words used to describe them—fantastical, morbid,

Tanaquil Le Clercq and Francisco Moncion in *La Valse*. New York City Ballet. Choreography by George Balanchine © The George Balanchine Trust. Photo, Jerome Robbins Dance Division, The New York Public Library for the Performing Arts, Astor, Lenox and Tilden Foundations.

perfumed, dream-like, atmospheric, haunted—suggest a kinship with this Ravel work. The haunted-ballroom atmosphere was always appealing to the mystical side of Balanchine, but what is interesting here is that these ballets of the 1930s are so clumped together in time that they suggest a phase. In later years Balanchine had no "phases" or "periods"; he much preferred contrast and variety, if only because he was intent on building a repertory. So how to account for this cycle of the misterioso in the 1930s? Perhaps one can attribute it to the influence of friends/collaborators at the time: Boris Kochno, who was brilliant at transforming fantasy into workable librettos; and Pavel Tchelitchev, a fabulist painter and theatrical designer. I feel that I am on thin ice again in this matter of influence; suffice it to say that within the next five years, Balanchine would not be influenced by anybody. Inspired, yes, by composers and dancers, but not influenced.

Among the Balanchine ballets that still exist, the nearest spiritual sister of *La Valse* would be *La Sonnambula* (1946), because it is a critique of a decadent society and has elements of the macabre. As pungent as *La Sonnambula* is, however, it has weak spots in the divertissement section. *La Valse*, on the other hand, sucks you into its eventual vortex from beginning to end (although there are a couple of moments where Balanchine loses his grip). In the last movement of *Bourrée Fantasque* he creates a whirlwind of festivity by having cadre upon cadre of dancers fly across the stage. Some dubbed these moments "organized chaos." Balanchine uses the same construct toward the end of *La Valse*, but in this ballet you want more chaos than organization. I have already described the passage where a woman leads two tidy rows of dancers in quick footwork. It's pretty, but generic—again, it's too organized. Lastly, the business of unison dancing. This is Balanchine's favorite way of doing finales, and I love them for their pizzazz. But with a corpse lying at the back of the stage, do we really want the waltzers doing a Broadway number? Especially considering the way the corpse got to the back of the stage. Many heroines have met their death in ballets, and their bodies are handled decorously so as to preserve their identities as dancers; that is, their arms are nicely placed and their feet pointed. In *La Valse* the dead woman is hauled away. You can feel the weight of her body; it's dead weight. I have always been startled by the almost gory nature of her last dance, as it were. It's as if Balanchine decided to strip the ballet of its irony. With a stroke of realism, he says that a dead arm has no alluring contours; a corpse is shapeless and death is ugly.

Ravel composed Valses Nobles et Sentimentales in 1911 and orchestrated it in 1912. La Valse, originally called Vienna in 1907, in honor of the nineteenth-century waltz, was orchestrated in 1920 and retitled La Valse. Diaghilev had commissioned this score but then rejected it for not being sufficiently theatrical. Here is one instance proving that Diaghilev's taste was not infallible, although it's true that the great choreographers Nijinska and Ashton achieved shaky results with the music. Balanchine's version continues to satisfy and delight in its morbid way.

The success of the ballet in its early years was partly due to the first woman in white, Tanaquil Le Clercq, whose innate sense of drama and glamour made her unsurpassable in the role. In 1956, when she was Balanchine's wife, she contracted polio, which ended her career, and Balanchine dropped the ballet. In 1962 he revived it for Patricia McBride, with coaching from Le Clercq herself. You might say that Le Clercq's willingness to look into the mirror of her past saved *La Valse* from death.

Scotch Symphony

1952

Throughout ballet history choreographers have fallen roughly into two camps: those who were most interested in dance expression itself, and those who wanted dance to comply with narrative logic and historical accuracy. The first put a premium on imagination; the second on dramatic integrity. In Balanchine's early years, while he was learning his craft in Russia, the debate coalesced around the figures of Marius Petipa and Michel Fokine. Petipa wanted to choreograph interesting divertissements and Fokine felt strongly that decor, costumes, and movement should all combine to reflect the nature of the story and the time in which it was set. In the ballet that first brought Petipa fame, *The Daughter of the Pharaoh*, the ballerina wore a tutu with hieroglyphic figures embroidered on it. Fokine used this ballet as his whipping post against Petipa. How ridiculous, Fokine wrote, to represent Egyptian culture with such a costume. For Petipa, being true to the heroine meant accurately reflecting not her nationality, but her rank: the heroine is a ballerina, and thus she must wear a tutu. She must not dance in the style of an Egyptian but like a ballerina, with virtuoso steps as defined by the ballet lexicon.

A ballet like *La Valse* would have won Fokine's approval, because all of its elements contribute harmoniously and logically to the point of the narrative. However, Balanchine obviously falls more within Petipa's aesthetic, and *Scotch Symphony* is a nice example of his paying little heed to dramatic unity or consistency. The first movement of the ballet (set to the second movement of Mendelssohn's Symphony No. 3, or Scottish symphony—Balanchine omitted the first movement) features a female lead. Brilliant in its footwork, it's an important part. Yet the kilt-wearing lassie never makes a return visit after the ballet's first movement. What happens to her? you might well ask. In the second, adagio movement we visit a sylph and her desirous cavalier, and though she appears again in the third and last section, she is no longer a sylph. She is a ballerina with the steps to prove it, and then a bride (or so I believe).

I am always astounded to hear people in the audience complain about these illogical turns of events, instead of enjoying them for the poetic license Balanchine loves to take. When *Scotch Symphony* was first danced in 1952, critics also complained and criticized the ballet's narrative structure in much the same terms Fokine used when he took Petipa to task. So the argument goes on. Sometimes, I admit, I too wish that Balanchine's ballets were more Fokinian, more unified. I think especially of *Chaconne*, which opens in the Elysian fields with appropriately dream-like choreography and then moves, as though nothing jarring had happened, into a neutral space for classical dancing. Perhaps the reason why leaps of place and style are troublesome in *Chaconne* is because the opening section's mood and choreography are unusual and indelible. Nothing in *Scotch Symphony* is as poetically intense; indeed, a good deal of the choreography per se, especially for the ensemble, is no more than serviceable. What holds us to the ballet is the rare glimpse it provides of a masterful choreographer of the twentieth century looking back on a masterpiece of the nineteenth, *La Sylphide*.

Scotch Symphony has two Highland themes, but the ballet carries them lightly, and that lightness of allusion to time and place accounts for the ballet's charm. Balanchine's interest in Scotland was piqued when the New York City Ballet danced at the Edinburgh Festival in August 1952. He saw there the famous nighttime military tattoo and loved the spectacle of it. Maria Tallchief, who accompanied him, writes in her autobiography that he "watched it with the rapt attention of a child" and talked about it for days after. He was also taken with Scotland's being the homeland of the sylph and of the great Romantic ballet *La Sylphide*. These inspirations

Kathryn Morgan and Robert Fairchild in *Scotch Symphony*. New York City Ballet. Choreography by George Balanchine © The George Balanchine Trust. Photo © by Costas.

he wedded to the Mendelssohn score, and the ballet premiered in November 1952 with Tallchief as the sylph and André Eglevsky her swain.

As for the tattoo, a few patches of marching steps sum up references to the ceremony, and sometimes the dancers curve their arms upward in a wide semicircle in the manner of Scottish and Irish folk dance. Balanchine later amplified the tattoo and the folk dances in *Union Jack*, in 1976. For *Scotch Symphony* he concentrated on the sylph story, which he developed in the second movement. The beauty of it is the way Balanchine pinpoints the essence of the relationship between the sylph and her admirer. Curling toward him and away, she beckons for him to follow her, but he can't possess her because her attendants block him. In other Romantic ballets or those in the romantic vein—the vision scene in *The Sleeping Beauty*,

Kathryn Morgan and Robert Fairchild in *Scotch Symphony*. New York City Ballet. Choreography by George Balanchine © The George Balanchine Trust. Photo
© by Costas.

for one, or Balanchine's own *Tschaikovsky Suite No. 3*—the attendants
are female, and in protecting the heroine they appear as a sisterhood. In
Scotch Symphony, however, the sylph's guard are men, dressed in the same
splendid kilts they wore in the first movement. Perhaps Balanchine thinks
of these tattoo-marching men as protectors of the realm, and of the sylph.
In any case, the delight of this section is to count the ways this honor
guard stymies the pursuer. Sometimes the retinue walks forcefully toward
him with outstretched arms. Hands off, they declare. Or they promenade
the sylph in a circle so that she has already sailed past him before he can
catch her. The loveliest moment is when her attendants cluster around her
as though protecting a precious rosebud. Her admirer runs to one side of
the stage, then the other. The rose and her thorns follow him with their

heads, but stand fast. Two men lift her high in the air and gently toss her into the arms of the cavalier, but as soon as she alights on his chest she slips away. (In *America's Prima Ballerina* Tallchief writes that the toss was meant to evoke the sylphs in the nineteenth century who flew across the stage on wires.)

Many of the passages are repeated verbatim; indeed, I can't think of another Balanchine work that has so many repetitions. True, the music repeats aplenty, but I think Balanchine follows suit because repetition generalizes the action, giving it the feel of ritual. But the third time the sylph beckons to the man to follow her, he refuses and pulls her back toward him. For some reason—his assertiveness?—she now decides to relinquish her sylph behavior. She pirouettes, he catches her, and off they go together.

Throughout the dance Balanchine eschews physical impersonation of the sylph as her images have come down to us through *La Sylphide*. Allegra Kent, one of the loveliest of Balanchine's *Scotch* sylphs, wondered if she was supposed to be a sylph at all. "There were theories," she says in Nancy Reynolds' *Repertory in Review*. "I was too sylphlike, not sylphlike enough. I was really a sylph; I was a girl pretending to be a sylph." Finally she followed Balanchine's advice and just danced it! The sylph's character, too, veers from the stereotype. Rather than being capricious, she is enigmatic and at one moment surprisingly tender, when she gently lifts one arm of her pursuer and then the other. Perhaps she is instructing him in how to be as graceful as she is. Perhaps she is teaching him how to fly!

The sylph transforms into a virtuoso dancer in the third, final movement—beats, pirouettes, sharp footwork—and her swain, now a standard cavalier, has his virtuoso moment in the sun as well. After a brief stint of mazurka steps (Fokine would be livid over this anachronism) the couple exits and Balanchine carries their exciting passages into the ensemble with jubilant lifts. The music quiets down in a gentle meandering interlude, and a new story slowly materializes, inspired by the suggestiveness of the score and Balanchine's receptivity to it. The ladies gather at one side of the stage and the men at the other. In the center of each cluster are the two principals. They sway back and forth to each other, and all then gather around the united couple, crisscrossing their arms above the principals' heads so as to form a canopy, and perhaps to bless them. The group reassembles into simple lines behind the main couple, at which point the music begins bold declarative statements, announcing and repeating the melody over and over. Balanchine hears in these repetitions a dialogue between the instruments: now it's my turn, now it's yours. In a charming replication of this conversation, the ballerina *développés* forward, and the ensemble follows suit; she moves into an attitude, and so does the ensemble; she is promenaded in attitude, and ditto for the group. Perhaps it is the ceremonial sound of Mendelssohn here that convinces me that marriage vows are taking place in front of a congregation. But as so often happens when a story materializes out of nowhere, you don't know if it's primarily the music or the choreography that makes it so.

At the end of the ballet, Balanchine brings back the tattoo marching to conclude on a celebratory note. The tattoo naturally brings back a memory of the first movement and the brio of its leading lady, especially as it was danced by Patricia Wilde, the original lassie. But there is really no place for her in the "wedding ceremony," for she is one of those Balanchine figures who, despite her good cheer (or maybe because of it), remains forever single. She's the girl next door. Of course, he could have brought her back for the tattoo, but the passage is too brief for her graceful reentry. It would be a stilted tying up of loose ends. Besides, Balanchine often likes loose ends.

Allegro Brillante

1956

Balanchine said that *Allegro Brillante* "contains everything I know about classical ballet—in thirteen minutes." This must be the most provocative description of a ballet he ever made, but would that he had said more! If compression was his intent for the ballet, it's no wonder that he put the dancers to work right away; as the curtain rises, the ensemble is already on the move, dancing in a pinwheel formation. As a display of ballet's possibilities—technically and architecturally—I wonder, though, if the first movement of *Ballet Imperial* (to Tchaikovsky's Piano Concerto No. 2) does not surpass *Allegro Brillante* (to Tchaikovsky's unfinished Piano Concerto No. 3). Or to put the comparison another way, *Allegro* might be a miniature version of *Ballet Imperial*. It has to be. *Ballet Imperial* has more than thirty dancers in its cast, whereas *Allegro* is staged for only four couples and a principal couple. With such a small cast, Balanchine cannot arrange the troops in the myriad patterns he arranges in *Ballet Imperial*. Nor can he subdivide them into several tiers of importance. So here are two common Balanchinian strategies missing from *Allegro*. But *Allegro* has a third favorite device that the larger ballet has not: the canon. As used in this ballet, the canon has the effect of doubling the size of the cast, creating a kind of hall of mirrors. I think especially of a long passage for the ensemble, early on, of quick small steps and, later, to the same melody, a part where those steps are repeated but with the principal

The New York City Ballet in *Allegro Brillante*. Choreography by George Balanchine © The George Balanchine Trust. Photo © by Costas.

woman dancing one beat ahead of the other four women. It all looks so much more complicated and populated than it is—and that's the point. The most exultant moment of the ballet, and the music, owes its power to a canon-like structure as well. The women step into arabesque on consecutive beats and then one by one fall way back into their partners' arms one, two, three, four! The moment resounds like cannon fire. The effect, which owes much to triumphant chords of the brass, is as grand as any moment in *Ballet Imperial*, and no matter how many times I have seen *Allegro* I experience its excitement as if for the first time. The marvel is that the feeling is created with such reduced means.

Allegro Brillante does a lot with a little. In this sense, it is an essay in craft, on working through a particular challenge. Balanchine admitted to finding problem-solving stimulating, but what the audience most keenly feels is the ballet's vigor. Tellingly, the dancers rarely stand in fifth position, which is closed and tight. Fourth position, which has a wider stance and thus more breadth, dominates. Sometimes fourth position has a spacious, airy effect, and sometimes, when the feet are solidly planted on the floor, it can be forceful. When the ballerina prepares for pirouettes—there are scads of them—she starts (or should start) from a very, very wide fourth position, with her back leg extended at least three feet behind the front. The effect is very, very forceful.

Those with an interest in the development of Balanchine's technique might suppose that these deep preparations for turning began with Suzanne Farrell, since she writes at length in her autobiography, *Holding On to the Air*, about Balanchine's challenging her to do them. Yet already in 1956, when *Allegro* was premiered and Farrell was still a kid, Balanchine was using these unorthodox preparations. Maria Tallchief, for whom the ballet was created, writes in her autobiography of this new element. "Because of the emphatic, almost exaggerated preparation, the turns gained a weighty, solid propulsion. . . . I think those swooping, lunging turns expressed the music's heart and pulse," she wrote.

The ballerina and cavalier first announce themselves with pauses in fourth position and other introductory movements, whereupon she plunges into huge *grands ronds de jambes* ending with deep arabesques *penchées*. Just as the very beginning of the ballet thrusts us right into the middle of things, so do the ballerina's first moves sweep us into a largeness of scale exhilarating for its boldness. More of the propulsion that Tallchief writes about is provided by the ensemble's fast entrances and exits—first the ladies, then the men, then the ladies. Sometimes when I imagine the ballet in my mind, I don't see it as much as feel gusts of air sweeping across the stage.

Following Tchaikovsky's moments of relaxed pace, Balanchine sometimes pulls back from the ballet's drive. In the music's most extended period of ease, the cavalier enters alone (walking, not running) and joins the ensemble in pretty tableaux. If one is still considering Balanchine's statement that the ballet is a compendium of everything he knows, the tableau is one element to add to the list. There are also smatterings of romantic gesture, which reflect lyrical interludes in the score. Yet he also inserts moments of romantic tenderness in a passage of music that is emphatically not lyrical: the main piano cadenza. Like the ballerina in the cadenza of *Ballet Imperial*, the ballerina here tears through the music with flashing pirouettes and brilliant jumps, yet in the middle of the fire she

Sofiane Sylve and Philip Neal in *Allegro Brillante*. New York City Ballet. Choreography by George Balanchine © The George Balanchine Trust. Photo © by Costas.

twice takes time out and runs to her partner on the side of the stage and embraces him. These are curious moments, these little footnotes of love. Sometimes they make me smile for seeming like afterthoughts: oh yes, I must not forget that my partner is watching me dance. Mostly, though, they are puzzling. *Allegro Brillante* is so unified in its vocabulary and consistent with the tone of the music that one false step is magnified.

The ballet slipped into the City Ballet's repertory on March 1, 1956, virtually unannounced. It was a substitute for a revival of Robbins' *The Guests*. Robbins could not rehearse because he was busy working on a Chopin ballet, which turned out to be *The Concert*. So as Balanchine sometimes had to do in those years, he whipped up a fill-in. *Allegro*

Brillante was no soufflé, however; it has remained a core part of the repertory, useful because of its small cast and scant production requirements and enduring for its exciting use of the classical vocabulary. The ballet's costumes were literally unannounced. They were designed by Karinska, but she received no credit on the program, for reasons I do not know. Yet Toni Bentley, in her book about Karinska, claims that the little chiffon dresses she created for the women were a debut of the genre and subsequently became a standard style. They became a balletic version of the little black dress.

Divertimento No. 15

Among many other things, *Agon* is an essay on the arithmetical possibilities of setting a ballet for twelve dancers. By the time the ballet is over, the illustrations of how twelve can be broken down into quartets, trios, duets, and so on achieve a theatrical power of their own. Arithmetic as drama also pervades *Divertimento No. 15*, which is set to Mozart's music of the same title. The source of drama is that the number of men and women are distributed unevenly. There are three men and five women. How Balanchine shapes Mozartian grace out of his unbalanced cast of principals is the sustaining impetus of the ballet.

The most extended display of the challenge Balanchine set for himself is in the long cadenza following the five pas de deux of the andante. With stately promenades and walks, he arranges a series of tableaux vivants so that the men can partner each woman without anyone being left out of the action for too long a time. As the dancers weave from background to foreground, and into trios and couples, there are sometimes one or two women standing on the side, unescorted. But then the men bring them forward in *bourrées*, and everything is right with the world. Tracking the dancers as they dissolve and evolve into ever-changing groupings is delightful recreation for those interested in Balanchine's craft. But of course there is more to the story than craft. Out of asymmetry can harmony be born.

This cadenza was composed in the mid-1960s by John Colman, a long-time rehearsal pianist for Balanchine. Following his instructions, Colman made it much longer than the one it supplanted, which had been arranged by Toscanini. You may surmise that Balanchine wanted his interlude for five and three to make a big impact. The five/three lineup comes into play as well in the second cadenza, just before the ballet ends. This one is short and less fluid musically as well as choreographically; I much prefer the amplitude with which Balanchine draws his social commentary in the first cadenza. (The critic Arlene Croce, on the other hand, thought that the prominence of the first cadenza undercut the second.)

The uneven number of male and female principals also gives the edge of surprise to all of *Divertimento*. You can never be sure how and when the ballerinas, especially, will be deployed. There is no grand entrance for any or all of them. Instead, Balanchine sprinkles them into the mix. The curtain opens to reveal two of them, standing in front of an ensemble of eight women. They dance little helloes to the audience and each other, then exit. A little later on, the three men enter with a touch of gravitas, and then three different ballerinas arrive. This trio shapes itself into two versus one, but when the three men and women then dance as couples, mark it in your memory; it is the first and last time that conventional pairings grace the stage. For after this sextet, the two other women run on, allowing Balanchine a short preview of the odd-ladies-out format.

In the last movement, the comings and goings of the principals make the section fairly bubble with surprise. One trio—two women flanking a man—gallops around the stage, and when they reach the front wing another woman takes the place of the first so quickly that you barely notice the swap—but you do notice it, and you smile. In this final movement, and in the first as well, the steps are bouncy, ebullient even, but what I find interesting is that Mozart's playfulness is expressed less by the steps than by the ballet's structural game—a sort of musical chairs without a winner. Even in the closing passage of the ballet Balanchine is busy making it all come out right. We find the men doing double duty as partners for the women in their pirouettes.

The andante (the fourth of the ballet's five sections) is a series of five pas de deux whose tone is determined by the five-and-three format. Because

Nichol Hlinka, Ethan Stiefel, and Jenifer Ringer in *Divertimento No. 15*. New York City Ballet. Choreography by George Balanchine © The George Balanchine Trust. Photo © by Costas.

the men must each partner more than one woman, there is no singular coupleness to the duets. Thus they proceed without the feelings of romance or sexual bond that characterize the majority of Balanchine's pas de deux. He once said that Mozart transcends emotion, that his music is cold, like ice cream. Ice cream is indeed cold, but it is also warm with cream and sugar and the tastiness of fruit. Perhaps this is what Balanchine meant when he turned Mozart's coldness into a paradox, but I do know that the duets are rich and flavorful and impersonal. Each of them is subsumed by the onward flow of the music. Although some are punctuated by a lift into the wings at the end, there are no beginnings and ends in the overall effect, and the fact that one couple's exit overlaps with the entrance of the next couple makes the entire movement all the more seamless. It just goes and goes and goes. All is calm, all is bright. And relaxed. For even though these duets are densely choreographed, with intricate promenades and lifts, there is always breathing room where the couple separates and "talk" quietly to each other with ports de bras and soft lunges. There is a center, though, to the long, seamless impetus of the dancing and music. It occurs in the third duet, when the music settles into what the critic Robert Garis called the "belly" of the andante. Balanchine marks it the way he usually marks the bellies of other scores. The ballerina does a *grand développé à la seconde*, and the ballerina who knows what she's doing indicates the importance of the movement by lifting her foot off the floor with special suppleness. (That suppleness is the payoff for the hours of practice that dancers did in Balanchine's classes, but the step's musical context is straight out of Petipa.) The difference between Petipa and Balanchine is that Petipa didn't choreograph to music as profound as Mozart's, and so the musical point that the third ballerina's *développé* makes is more potent.

It's curious that Balanchine did not give that duet to the leading woman of the five—if there is, in fact, such a figure. To a limited extent, there is, although it's possible to miss the special status. In its heart, *Divertimento* proclaims equality among the five ladies. Yet when five of them dance in a line, the same woman always stands in the center. In the cadenzas, it's the same woman who occupies the center of the various formations, whether dancing or at rest. And although in the andante each couple enters together, in the fifth pas de deux the man and woman enter from opposite sides of the stage. It's the almost-lead ballerina who receives this special introduction.

Her solo in the preceding theme and variations is also special for its electrifying speed. When it's done right, sparks fly! Each of the other variations has particular coloration, too. The first, for two men, is noble in its spaciousness and simplicity (and is one of my favorite moments of the ballet). The second is perky; the fourth, bold for its large *battements*. On the whole, though, the variations move along as the duets do in the andante—seamlessly. The dance public has come to expect a series of variations to be cameo portraits of personality as suggested by the music, the model being the fairies' variations in the prologue of *The Sleeping Beauty*. But in *Divertimento* Balanchine is listening not to Tchaikovsky's attention to narrative concerns but to Mozart's long arc of music.

There is one moment, though, where *Beauty*'s light shines on the Mozart. This happens at the end of the andante, when all eight principals form a line and link arms. The women extend their legs forward in *développé* and then bring them to the back in arabesque *penchée*. The sumptuousness of the tableau is a dead ringer for the various tableaux for the fairies, and the feeling they bring in both ballets is pretty much the same. What had been separate entities are now joined as one, gathered in celestial grace. This coming together in the Mozart is one of those instances where you can't be sure if the music told Balanchine what to do, or whether Balanchine's choreography makes us hear the music as a joining of hands. Is Balanchine reflecting Mozart, or is Mozart reflecting Balanchine? Whatever you make of the question, this moment defines the meaning of ensemble.

The idea of ensemble in this ballet flows from the seamlessness of the variations and duets and takes several forms. Sometimes the sense of ensemble provides closure to a section. At the end of the theme and variations all eight principals return to the stage. The two men who had first iterated the theme repeat their lambent ports de bras and soft *tombés*; then all bow and exit. One of the most beautiful and poignant moments of the whole ballet comes at the end of the andante. After the cadenza, the men and the women each form a tight circle and raise their arms high. Perhaps they are offering a toast to Mozart. Yet the moment runs deeper. They seem to be marking the experience of dancing together. The intimacy of it is felt all the more keenly when, in the next moment, the dancers regroup into a more formal and public shape: two lines. They solemnly bow to each other across the broad space of the stage, pivot, and exit. It is not uncommon for Balanchine to conclude an extended pas de deux with bows. The gesture bespeaks courtesy, but it also describes Balanchine's description of Mozart's music, as being as cold as ice cream. Underlying the formality of the bow is a tacit recognition of the richness that has come before.

There is in *Divertimento* an ensemble in the conventional sense as well; that is, eight women function as a corps de ballet to the principals. It's the corps that carries the minuet, the third section of the ballet. (The score contains a second minuet, but Balanchine didn't use it; nor did he use the

New York City Ballet dancers near the end of the andante in *Divertimento No. 15*. Choreography by George Balanchine © The George Balanchine Trust. Photo © by Costas.

opening andante of the finale.) I find this minuet rather four-square and dry, and overly tied to the minuet rhythm. The eight ladies have more fun at the beginning of the finale, when they bound onstage two by two. They also provide pictorial support for the principals with their ports de bras. This is standard stuff in a Balanchine ballet. What's a little different here is that sometimes, especially in the finale, the corps' arm movements seem to be cheering the principals on. As the leads gallop around the stage in their always-changing configurations, the corps dancers wave their arms and tilt their heads from side to side in especially close coordination with the music's beat and happy spirit. In one passage the ballerinas seem to cheer each other on as well. It's when the five of them at last dance together in a line. One by one they break out of the line and dance solo in stage center, while their compatriots keep time with their arms. In my mind's ear I hear them clapping to egg the soloist on, and at an especially joyous performance I imagine them all jamming to Mozart.

Croce quipped that *Divertimento No. 15* is one of those ballets that are famous for not being done well. My experience with it would prompt me to amend that to "not done well enough." I often feel this way about many ballets, but *Divertimento* offers special challenges. For proof, you need only think of the superb dancers on whom Balanchine set it. In the first version of 1952, called *Caracole,* the leads were Diana Adams, Melissa Hayden, Tanaquil Le Clercq, Maria Tallchief, Patricia Wilde, André Eglevsky, Nicholas Magallanes, and Jerome Robbins. In 1956, for the Mozart Festival of the American Shakespeare Festival in Stratford, Connecticut, Balanchine made a more or less new version (how much more and how much less is open to question). He replaced the enchanting title *Caracole* with the workaday name still used today, but the starry lineup of ballerinas remained intact, except that the young and immensely talented Allegra Kent replaced Tallchief. The men were Magallanes again, and Herbert Bliss and Roy Tobias, all of principal rank. The ballet needs not only extraordinary talent but much preparation time. As a result it had, until recent years, a performance history of now you see me, now you don't. The worst of it was when it was canceled at the last minute, to groans from the audience.

Whatever the caliber of performance, one is grateful to have *Divertimento* around, for itself of course, but also because it is the only Mozart piece in the City Ballet's active repertory. In all, Balanchine made some dozen pieces to Mozart. The first, made in the 1930s, was a duet danced at a party at the Plaza hotel's Persian Room in New York. Many other dances were similarly occasional or created for operas. *Symphonie Concertante,* from 1945, was dropped from the City Ballet repertory in the 1950s, and though it was picked up by American Ballet Theatre in 1984, its performance record there is sporadic, since ABT is not a custodian of Balanchine's work. And, as it turns out, the one survivor in stable condition, *Divertimento,* was born by chance. In 1952 Balanchine was planning on doing a Don Juan ballet to the Richard Strauss score. He began rehearsals, but the score, he wrote in his *Complete Stories of the Ballets,* "could not accommodate the ideas I had in mind"—whatever that means. Needing a substitute premiere for the season, he turned to the Mozart divertimento, which he had always loved, and cooked up a ballet in one week. We owe Richard Strauss our gratitude.

Sometimes I wonder why Balanchine did not make another Mozart piece in the 1960s, when the City Ballet was flooded with new talent. More often I wonder why there is not more Mozart, period. And while I'm on the subject, why not more Bach or Schumann, or any Schubert or Beethoven? Balanchine's public opinions on composers are scant, but he often said that the music he favored for choreography was "musique dansante." The list was short: Tchaikovsky, Delibes, and Stravinsky. His preference for dance music did not preclude his use of a huge range of composers, but I think he was wary of the so-called great music. Maybe he had good reason. His one Bach ballet, *Concerto Barocco*, is a masterpiece, while his work to an orchestration of Bach, by Webern, for the ballet *Episodes* has a troublesome tone. *Divertimento No. 15* is one of his best, but *Symphonie Concertante* is flawed. It was created for students, and with its starched, academic use of the ensemble it looks it. Perhaps he felt that much music was best left in the concert hall, that he had nothing to add to musical masterpieces. Perhaps he was right. *Divertimento* realizes everything that is exquisite in the music, but I don't think his choreography adds to one's pleasure in it, in that it does not reveal hidden structures or tonalities or even emotions. As perfect as the music is, it did not stir Balanchine's imagination. If anything, it prompted a kind of correction, which was to cut on the bias Mozart's balance and proportion with an off-balance cast of five ballerinas and three cavaliers.

Stars and Stripes

1958

As preposterous as the reaction seems today, *Stars and Stripes* raised a few eyebrows when it premiered in January 1958. How could Balanchine choreograph to Sousa? Whether the question was born out of curiosity or skepticism, he was put on the defensive. Remember, only two months earlier he had worked hand in hand with Stravinsky in creating *Agon*, a landmark of modernity in music and dance. The fact that Balanchine had recently gone out of the concert hall for *Western Symphony*, in 1954, was evidently forgotten. Or perhaps the associations connected with Western folk tunes were more congenial than with military marching bands. Balanchine parried the Sousa question in several ways. To the ignorant, he presented Sousa's bona fides: he was an accomplished violist and a student of Offenbach. To the snobs he said, "I like Sousa. He makes me feel good." And I say, Bravo Balanchine!

Like its sibling, *Western Symphony*, *Stars and Stripes* falls into the category of Americana. But unlike the pointedly American ballets of the 1930s and 40s by other choreographers—Ruth Page's *Frankie and Johnny*, Eugene Loring's *Billy the Kid*, Agnes de Mille's *Rodeo*, and Jerome Robbins' *Fancy Free*, to name a few—Balanchine did not attempt to Americanize classical language with vernacular gesture. His method was less radical and, with the exception of *Fancy Free*, more enduring. He keeps the classical technique he uses in most all of his work but flavors it with references inspired by his chosen music. Sousa's band music makes Balanchine see drum majorettes, spiffy cadets, and a bugle-blowing ballerina. They are on parade. You don't have to love America to love this ballet, but you do have to love parades. There are more long lines in *Stars and Stripes* than in any other ballet. And march they do, the ladies' legs springing into *passés* as happily as for the myriad *passés* in *Symphony in C*, except that in *Stars* the raised leg is turned in, marching style—and Broadway style.

Balanchine uses the turned-in *passé* when he wants to go modern, as in his many Stravinsky ballets. He also uses it to impart a jazzy look, and more broadly to evoke the world of popular entertainment. Broadway was his home base during the 1930s and 40s, a time when other choreographers were busy on the concert stage giving ballet an American accent, be it through subject matter or dance language itself. The era in which he worked on Broadway is still alive in his ballets, which in a sense dates them, but which also accounts for the blithe spirit of his jazzy pieces. You can't see it more clearly than in those turned-in *passés*. In Balanchine's hands, the body's configuration is sexy but also demure. Just consider the line of a Bob Fosse dancer. Her legs are splayed so that our eye focuses on her pelvis. In *Stars*—or in *Rubies* or *Who Cares?*—there are no pelvises glaring at us; there is instead the beguiling curve of the thigh as it turns inward from the hip.

The charm of Balanchine's Broadway is intact in *Stars*, but in this one he also branches out to other forms of mass entertainment. So there are brief spells of Rockette kicking, though with a Balanchine imprint: the girls kick their legs at a faster clip. He also tosses acrobatics into the mix. The soloist in the first "campaign," as each of the five movements of the ballet is called, hoists her leg sky-high with one of her hands, and trying to look as elegant as she possibly can, *relevés* up and down on her standing leg as she moves across the stage in front of her regiment. In the finale this ungainly—some would say vulgar—maneuver reappears, but in a context that is one of the ballet's most inspired moments. As Hershy Kay's orchestration of Sousa turns mellow, evoking wheat stirring in the breeze, the entire cast does a *revérence* straight out of the halls of the Imperial theater in Russia, as if in celebration of our beautiful American landscape. Next minute, they're doing the leg-hoist thing. In the blink of an eye we move from the Old World to the New. Balanchine's choice of emblem for the New World is so cheeky it makes me beam.

Balanchine liked to describe himself as an entertainer. In almost all of his ballets the entertainer and the artist is not an either/or proposition. He is both, which is one reason why Balanchine is often compared to Shakespeare, whose plays thrived in the commercial world of Elizabethan theater. *Stars and Stripes* is unusual in that the entertainment factor is paramount. As far as its structure goes, I am always struck by its simplicity and repetitiveness. The first three campaigns—set to "Corcoran Cadets," "Rifle Regiment," and "Thunder and Gladiator," and each for an ensemble of twelve and a soloist—start out in pyramid formation, with everyone dancing together for a long time. Then the group breaks up into smaller units, allowing for solo dancing, and then it regroups back into the pyramid. Absent are the ingenious, ever-changing patterns. The patterns he does choose are flashy and simple—long lines, big circles of turning dancers, and of course the pyramid. Only in the third campaign, which is for men, does Balanchine do something "artistic" with the pyramid. The men start dancing on a diagonal, which makes us see the formation from a new perspective: the front line is suddenly five men instead of one (the soloist).

But then this whole section is so razzle-dazzle that it makes considerations of artistry irrelevant. Kay begins "Thunder and Gladiator" with drum rolls, to which the men bound onto the stage line by line in big, traveling jumps. Once they are all assembled and the drums give way to melody, they tear into a cascade of turns and jumps, all of them flecked with crisp beats of their legs. Your adrenaline rush subsides for a bit when the group breaks into units of three, four, and five and when the orchestration thins out, too, favoring winds instead of brass. The trio moves in a charming canon and the quartet's leaps are more spacious. Your heart begins to pump again as the five remaining men of the ensemble fly into stage center and then out with soaring *cabrioles*. This moment has always been especially delicious for me, and I'm not certain why. Perhaps it's because they move in overlapping sequences as Kay's orchestration broadens to include the whole orchestra, so that you feel a groundswell of energy. Soon the whole bunch are whizzing around the stage in a circle (again),

Merrill Ashley in *Stars and Stripes*. New York City Ballet. Choreography by George Balanchine © The George Balanchine Trust. Photo © by Costas.

ending up in a pyramid (again). Accompanied by more drum rolls, which mimic the circus's musical cue that an especially dangerous stunt is happening, the men do that precarious virtuoso step: the double *tour en l'air*, not once but four times! Because the jumps are done in unison, the stakes are all the more high; one bad apple looks worse when surrounded by good apples. When they then march off, saluting the audience as they file by, you want to salute them back. Mission accomplished. Even if one or two didn't land from their double *tours* in a perfect fifth position.

Stars was the last of a quartet of new ballets to premiere within two months of each other. *Square Dance* and *Agon* came first, in November 1957, followed by *Gounod Symphony* and the Sousa opus in January 1958.

Sara Mearns, Charles Askegard, and the full cast in the closing of *Stars and Stripes.* New York City Ballet. Choreography by George Balanchine © The George Balanchine Trust. Photo © by Costas.

This remarkable outpouring of creativity had been preceded by a year of tragedy for Balanchine. His wife, Tanaquil Le Clercq, had been stricken by polio in the fall of 1956, and Balanchine spent the following months in Copenhagen, where she took ill, and Warm Springs, Georgia, caring for his wife and slowly accepting the fact that she would not be able to dance (or even walk) ever again. One can only imagine what this enforced layoff from work did to his own spirit, but once he was able to choreograph again, he did so with a magnificent vengeance.

I don't remember journalists noting this eruption of creative energy at the time (though it is duly acknowledged now), but I do remember their making a fuss about a smaller but important matter. The third, "Thunder and Gladiator" campaign in *Stars* proved emphatically that the City Ballet now had a strong male wing. The company always had terrific female virtuosos, but André Eglevsky had to carry the male banner alone. Now the young Jacques d'Amboise was on the scene. For him and Melissa Hayden, Balanchine fashioned in the ballet's fourth campaign a spectacular pas de deux to the marches "Liberty Bell" and "El Capitan." It is a traditional pas de deux in that it follows the conventional format of a formal duet succeeded by solos for each dancer and a coda. More importantly, it presents the ballerina as we know her from the nineteenth century. She is quick and delicate and precise in her footwork. To add to her piquancy, her head gets into the act when in her first solo she jauntily cocks it from side to side in between poses in attitude. The duet also has all the earmarks of the *grand pas de deux*: supported turns, promenades, elegant *développés* and arabesques. It's when the solos start that the section becomes the last word in pyrotechnics. The man's jumps and pirouettes and the woman's splits in the air make you cheer, but it's the overlapping succession of solos that brings you to the edge of your seat.

Like *Western Symphony, Stars and Stripes* rests on a humorous conceit, the joining of classical vocabulary with popular music. Balanchine once said that if you're joking you must be doubly serious. The duet in *Stars* is serious business indeed, yet it offers opportunities for the dancers to embellish the choreography with jokes. One of the standard ones is when the ballerina is turning in arabesque and the man must keep stepping back to avoid getting hit by her leg. (In an interview in Francis Mason's *I Remember Balanchine*, d'Amboise describes the moment as one he remembered from an earlier pas de deux that Balanchine made for a television program in 1952 called "One, Yuletide Square." An abridged version of *Coppélia*, it featured Tanaquil Le Clercq as Swanilda, Robert Helpmann as Dr. Coppélius, and Harpo Marx as one of the dolls. D'Amboise claims that about a third of the *Stars* duet was lifted from the television show.) Hayden was advised by Balanchine to play it straight, yet she confesses that it was hard not to inject "funny bits." How could a dancer resist the temptation to ham it up when her first entrance is accompanied by a warbling tuba? Obviously, dancers must use good judgment in how far to take the humor, but for the most part the choreography itself keeps them on the high ground. As it does for the entire ballet.

Stars does not attitudinize about its subject. Sousa does make us feel good, and the affection with which Balanchine treats the music and the majorettes, with their sweet white anklet socks, is so sincere as to convince the most skeptical. Except during the Vietnam War, when the company put the ballet into storage. The public simply couldn't swallow its patriotic spirit. But even during the one or two outings that the ballet had during the war, I, for one, fell hook, line, and sinker for the closing passage of the fifth campaign, set to "Stars and Stripes." Kay slows the march down with loud, emphatic chords, as if to announce that something new and wondrous is about to happen. It does. As the entire cast moves forward with jazzy *grands battements*, the flag unfurls from the ground and rises up, up, up like the Christmas tree in *The Nutcracker*. The fact that it ascends rather than descends is the key, I think, to the glory of the moment. For the flag takes your heart with it, rising ever upward toward the sky.

Episodes

1959

Balanchine was sometimes tipped off to interesting, unfamiliar music by Stravinsky's associate, Robert Craft. In 1952 Webern came through the pipeline to Balanchine, who was immediately intrigued. Seven years later he finally got the chance to choreograph to Webern's orchestral music in a ballet called *Episodes*. He chose five compositions, concluding with the Ricercata, Webern's orchestration of a part of The Musical Offering by Bach. Following on the heels of difficult music—astringent, unmelodious, each part of unnervingly brief duration—the Ricercata was obviously intended by Balanchine as a reconciliation, a coming together between two very different times and kinds of music. Maybe it was also a peace offering, for the choreography for the Ricercata is easy to read visually whereas the preceding sections are not.

The idea of reconciliation, of joining opposites, was actually a central conceit in the original conception of the complete *Episodes*. The work premiered on May 14, 1959, at a time when the worlds of modern dance and ballet were still wary of each other. The first section was choreographed by Martha Graham. Her contribution, to Webern's Passacaglia and Six Pieces, told the story of the rivalry between Mary Queen of Scots and Queen Elizabeth; Graham herself danced the role of Mary. But Graham's portion of *Episodes* dropped out of the New York City Ballet's repertory after two seasons, and the *Episodes* we see today is all Balanchine—minus one long solo he had made for Paul Taylor, then a member of Graham's troupe.

In 1959 the very idea of two heads of state sharing the same stage was extraordinarily newsworthy considering the temper of the times. Perhaps this is why Lincoln Kirstein thought up the idea in the first place: it would sell tickets. He also had a less benign motive: to reveal Graham, in her collaboration with Balanchine, as the lesser of the artists. "We gave her a long rope," Kirstein used to say years later with conspiratorial winks and chuckles.

Kirstein proposed the idea to Graham and Balanchine at an expensive restaurant in Manhattan. According to Agnes de Mille (in *Martha: The Life and Work of Martha Graham*), Graham was not enthusiastic about the idea and suspected that Balanchine was not either. However, she felt a certain loyalty to the embattled friendship she had with Kirstein. As for Balanchine, he was going to try his hand with Webern, and that is what counted most. His feelings about working with Graham remained off the record, though he did quip to Kirstein that perhaps the City Ballet could be renamed Chock Full of Nuts. In the original plan, many more hands were to cross the ocean than actually did. In the end, Balanchine used only one Graham dancer (Taylor) and Graham used only one ballet dancer (Sallie Wilson as Elizabeth), plus two men in minor parts. During the rehearsal period Graham discovered that she needed more music, to accommodate what many considered the highlight of her dance, a stylized tennis match between Elizabeth and Mary. Balanchine gave her the music he had been using for a pas de deux, the Six Pieces, and used the Five Pieces instead for the duet. That's about it for a sharing of resources.

As I remember the premiere, there was much expectation in the audience before the curtain went up, and a certain justified nervousness, as though a competition were about to take place. Graham received a small ovation at the beginning and a larger one at the end. I remember no such display for the Balanchine segment, but then there were no great personages or great moments in the ballet section to respond to. The fact is that Balanchine's *Episodes* was mostly puzzling and unsettling, even with the final tribute to Bach. The greater problem, of course, was absorbing this non-collaborative collaboration, this comparison between apples and oranges. You wondered: How come, and what for?

Some critics commented on the ironical underside of the endeavor. The "conservative" mode, ballet, seemed more avant-garde than the supposedly more radical modern dance. But these critics were talking about movement per se. If you were to rethink the comparison in terms of theatrical imagination, then Graham might have won. At the heart of her *Episodes* were the moments when Mary and Elizabeth magically slipped out of their elaborate ceremonial dresses, which were left to hang as skeletons, and then danced in simple dresses, symbols of their inner souls. The idea, as I remember it and as it is described eloquently by de Mille, among others, is breathtaking.

Perhaps the only part of Balanchine's *Episodes* to match Graham's in terms of theatrical wizardry was the sight of the large, muscular Paul Taylor tying himself into Balanchine's knots in the long solo, now absent. (City Ballet dancer Peter Frame learned the solo from Taylor in the mid-1980s, but performed it only for a while.) Taylor writes with great intelligence in his autobiography, *Private Domain*, about learning that solo and practicing it intensively on his own. He needed to adapt the connections between movements, which felt arbitrary to him, to the particular way in which his body moved. In the process, he hoped to discover the underlying idea of the solo, which he intuited was there. (Would that every dancer could grasp that every Balanchine dance has an underlying idea.) But he had trouble on that count, and one day asked Balanchine for guidance. Balanchine said "like a fly in a glass of milk," and Taylor was home free. "The picture was perfect," Taylor wrote. "The convoluted dance, resembling the buzzing circles of something subhuman caught within a deadly vortex of its own making, seemed to be an epigram about self-ordained patterns and death."

So who said that Balanchine didn't choreograph stories? In fact, *Episodes* does have a dramatic line. It culminated in Taylor's solo, which referred back to the several pas de deux set to the Five Pieces. These five terribly short episodes—the fourth no more than a few seconds—are miniature illustrations of how the man and woman make no sustainable contact.

Jason Fowler and Teresa Reichlen in the Five Pieces section of *Episodes*. New York City Ballet. Choreography by George Balanchine © The George Balanchine Trust. Photo © by Costas.

The coup de theatre, of course, is the episode in which their fusion metamorphoses them into a monster—a man with huge antlers growing out of his shoulders. The other parts are more connected to Taylor's image of a deadly vortex; the more entangled the man and woman become, the farther apart they are. Then, too, each section ends in mid-sentence, which is not as grotesque as the antler image, but is as unnerving for its lack of resolution. In each case, the woman puts herself in an awkward position (bent over on one foot) and is left there. End of story. To say that she is abandoned would be too humanizing. She is not abandoned. She is just there. These moments are cold, unfathomable. The audience doesn't

Likolani Brown, Albert Evans, Wendy Whelan (upside down), and Lauren King in the Concerto section of *Episodes*. New York City Ballet. Choreography by George Balanchine © The George Balanchine Trust. Photo © by Costas.

know if it's watching a tragic comedy or comic tragedy. Hence the titters you hear today and which occurred at the premiere (to Taylor's dismay).

The first part of *Episodes* is set to Webern's Symphony. It is a clean, fairly neutral exposition of the style Balanchine will use throughout. We've seen the angularities, inversions (most astonishing when the principal woman does *entrechats* upside down in the air), and pristine isolation of body parts before—in *Agon*, of course, and also in *The Four Temperaments*. What makes *Episodes* stranger than the earlier ballets is Webern. With a score devoid of rhythmic vitality, the choreography seems detached from the world; it is suspended in time and space, like "molecules," as Balanchine once described the music. The dancing begins with the ritual offering of hands, moves into the feet, and then into the whole body. Clarity of execution is everything, especially the way the flat foot leaves and returns to the floor; indeed, watching the Symphony section, you can understand why Balanchine paid so much attention to *battement tendu* in class. There are many repeats; the choreographic pulse is even, deliberate. The dancers' crystalline execution is what gives the section its energy.

From this exposition of technique and style, Balanchine hurtles us into Five Pieces, the nightmarish pas de deux in five slices. The following section, the Concerto, returns to the opening in its movement style but with a difference. Now there is a relationship between the man and the woman. Whereas the Symphony stresses clarity, the Concerto stresses the woman's flexibility, and it's her willingness to let her limbs be moved in extremis that suffuses her being with drama. She is compliant, obliging, and, most striking of all, both participant and observer of the manipulations; that is, she sometimes watches her leg being moved as though it isn't hers. In the beginning of the central pas de deux she is rather like the "doll" Swanilda in *Coppélia*, but without her agenda. By the end she attains a dignity for never resisting. The partnering in this section foreshadows the duets in *Stravinsky Violin Concerto* and *Duo Concertant*. In all three, Balanchine wanted to show us how a woman can consent to being a tool without relinquishing her spirit.

In its original form, with the Taylor solo, *Episodes* would have swerved, after the Concerto, into the bizarre once again, giving the ballet more vivid contrasts than it has now. As it presently plays, the ballet slides directly into the resolution, the Ricercata. Without the Taylor solo there is obviously less to be resolved, but certainly the dancers' harmonious lines and, above all, Webern's more sustained lines mark a return to normality. Yet this is the weakest part of the ballet. With an ensemble of fourteen, the stage is much fuller than in the previous sections, yet it falls short of the music's grandeur. Perhaps Balanchine wanted to go the less-is-more route, but the ending, when the dancers counter the music's swelling chords by standing with their arms at their sides and feet in parallel position, is simplicity overstated. Some have noted a preachy quality in the choreography, about the return to roots and all that. I tend to agree, and suspect that it comes from an overemphasis on architecture—on the effect of blocks of bodies moving in counterpoint, in the manner of Doris Humphrey—and an underemphasis on steps. I think that a more complex texture in movement vocabulary would have eased the didactic tone.

Nevertheless, the Ricercata is the one extant part of *Episodes* where you get the point. The five spooky pas de deux also play well—relatively speaking, but relative to what? In writing about this ballet I am amazed to find myself having to draw upon memories of the original cast in order to get a handle on its dramatic underpinnings. I don't think I could write that the Five Pieces is unfathomable—which is to say, like life itself—without remembering a sphinx-like Diana Adams and Jacques d'Amboise. Or that the Swanilda figure in the Concerto attains dignity without having in mind Allegra Kent's tenderness and curiosity about the wayward paths of her body. Or that the Symphony's drive derives from technical clarity without remembering Violette Verdy's electrified limbs. *Episodes*, you'd think, is not the kind of ballet whose viability is so intertwined with the dancers for whom it was created. Other ballets come more readily to mind: *Jewels*, for instance, or *Liebeslieder Walzer*. Yet these ballets today are much less a shell of their former selves than *Episodes*. But *Episodes* is a special case because of its music. It needs the mediation of dancers to bring the audience closer to the dance.

Monumentum Pro Gesualdo

In choosing repertory for the New York City Ballet, Balanchine was driven primarily by music. Lincoln Kirstein, on the other hand, was on the lookout for programming ideas that would add "spice," as he wrote, to the company's increasingly long seasons in New York. There was much spice in 1959–60, beginning in 1959 with *Episodes*, the company's outreach gesture to "the house opposite" of Martha Graham. In 1960 Kirstein's efforts to endow the City Ballet with cultural and intellectual luster went global. In January the company presented a program devoted to Latin American composers—eight ballets gathered under the title "Pan America." Writing in *Thirty Years: The New York City Ballet*, Kirstein acknowledged the political value in honoring Latin America: the region was of long-standing interest to Nelson Rockefeller, a patron of the company and the governor of New York at the time. The premiere in April of one of the most elaborate works Balanchine ever devised, *The Figure in the Carpet*, coincided with the opening of the Fourth International Congress of Iranian Art and Archeology in New York. Although the ballet received as much attention for its philosophical libretto as for its choreography, its production requirements, which included a working fountain, were too complicated and expensive to ensure a long performance life. It quickly became one of Balanchine's famous "lost" works. The two new works to survive the test of time were the most modestly conceived and least newsworthy. One was *Donizetti Variations*. The other was *Monumentum Pro Gesualdo*, which slipped into the final international bill, a salute to Italy, in November 1960.

A mere whisper of a ballet in regard to tone and length, it did nonetheless have the distinction of having a score by Stravinsky, and a newly born one at that. Stravinsky wrote it in the spring of 1960 and conducted its premiere that September at La Fenice in Venice, in honor of the 400th birthday of the Renaissance madrigalist Don Carlo Gesualdo. That's how it figured in the all-Italian program. Despite the Stravinsky factor, though, one can only wonder how this chamber ballet held its own against its other Italian compatriots on the program: the glamourously gothic *La Sonnambula*, set to Rieti's reworking of Bellini arias; the farcical *Con Amore*, by Lew Christensen to Rossini; and the dizzy *Donizetti Variations*. In the middle of all this commotion was *Monumentum Pro Gesualdo*, serene, above the fray, and short.

The score uses only three of Gesualdo's madrigals, which Stravinsky refashioned for orchestra. It adds up to about seven or eight minutes of dance. To this day, the brevity of the ballet still startles me. So accustomed are we to a dance of at least fifteen minutes' duration (maybe ten or twelve for a pas de deux) that anything less is disorienting. Since 1966 *Monumentum* has been paired with Stravinsky's *Movements for Piano and Orchestra*, yielding a "proper" chunk of time for a ballet. But the pairing still doesn't quell my disquiet when the curtain falls on *Monumentum*, even though the dancers sit in utter repose in a tableau that clearly spells "the end."

One source of disquiet, apart from length, is the music. Its muted horns and wind instruments, slightly dissonant, suggest to me a feeling of menace underneath the heavenly sound of the strings. Kirstein heard the music in a similar way. He wrote in a program note that the ballet "evokes the deliberate, almost sinister gravity and fatality shadowing court dances performed in the lifetime of this prince of madrigalists and murderers." Yes, Gesualdo was a murderer, of his wife and wife's lover and possibly of a child as well. Who knows if Stravinsky was indeed influenced by Gesualdo's biography when he wrote the music. As for me, my reading of *Monumentum* is influenced by my biography of Balanchine-watching.

I did not see *Monumentum* until after I had seen *Don Quixote* in 1965. In *Don Quixote* there is a powerful scene in which the Don, at the Spanish court, is humiliated by the nobility. All the while that they are bowing and promenading and waving their fans and feathers with courtly elegance, they are lobbing the Don's face with cream, almost blinding him. The memory of this depiction of evil lurking under the surface of good manners seeped into my feeling about the Stravinsky piece, because in this, too, the dancers move with stately grace and Renaissance flourish. The more courtly the *Monumentum* choreography is at any given moment, the more I smelled corruption. Today that association between the two ballets has evaporated. The darker aspects of the music are still there, but they only add mystery to the ballet's atmosphere. The ballet dwells in a world of hermetic breathlessness, adding its own sense of mystery to the music.

The most salient fact about this ballet is that it is slow. The dancers—a principal couple and six ensemble couples—move with grave deliberateness, whether simply walking, which they do a lot of, or doing more elaborate things. (When Suzanne Farrell was asked, during a video shoot about her coaching for the Interpreters Archive, which was harder to dance, *Monumentum* or the more acrobatic and musically difficult *Movements for Piano and Orchestra*, she implied that the former was. Moving slowly is difficult for today's dancers, she said.) Although the women wear short white tunics, the slow, measured pace of the movement sometimes suggests that they could be in long, heavy gowns. At one point in the second madrigal, the ballerina swishes her leg and arms in a quick circle, as if to brush her train out of the way. She ends the phrase in a high arabesque, a moment of triumph. The slow tempo also affects the way the canonic structure so dear to Balanchine plays out. Usually Balanchine has the ensemble repeat a phrase one or two beats behind the principals, in order to inject sparkle or wit into the stage picture. The canons in *Monumentum*, especially the ones in the first part, create a sense of water rippling by. The overall action is busy but gentle. In the third part the dancers move forward and back from their initial diagonal line also in canonic sequences, and here the effect is of a tide slowly surging forward and then receding. The image of receding is especially resonant in the final moment of the

Ask la Cour and Teresa Reichlen in *Monumentum Pro Gesualdo*. New York City Ballet. Choreography by George Balanchine © The George Balanchine Trust. Photo © by Costas.

ballet, when the women sink into splits and then softly bend their front legs toward them so that they form a right angle to their torsos.

If *Monumentum* were a painting, you could describe it as a white canvas with outcroppings of color. The most dramatic of them are the four times the ballerina is tossed high in the air between her partner and two other attendants; all of a sudden her weighted figure hangs suspended in the air. There are other patches of color, too: when she poses in high attitudes or falls off-balance in a deep arabesque. Still other figures pierce the whiteness not because of their scale but because of their inventiveness. As a dance phrase slowly works its way down the chain of command in canons, the women lean deeply into their partners' arms and are pivoted slowly in a circle, their feet poised not on full pointe, which would be conventional, but on three-quarters pointe. How haunting is that three-quarter lift in the foot. Another exquisite moment happens at the end of the first part. The ballerina walks in three increasingly small circles until she faces her partner's back. As he slowly kneels, she slides down his back until she rests on the floor, nestled in the crook of his back leg. Their arms rise slowly to the strings' song. I guess Balanchine knew that he had come up with a sublime maneuver, because he gives the couple plenty of air. The ensemble is absolutely still.

These moments evolve out of the general fabric of the ballet and of the music as well. The big tosses and other large movements coincide with Stravinsky's strong use of the horns, for example. But there are other events that seem to spring out of nowhere, or to put it more accurately, out of the inner sanctum of Balanchine's mind. Such a moment is when

Sean Lavery and Suzanne Farrell in *Monumentum Pro Gesualdo*. New York City Ballet. Choreography by George Balanchine © The George Balanchine Trust. Photo © by Costas.

the dancers cup their ears, as if listening to the music or their own inner voices. Naturally, the Prelude in *Les Sylphides* comes to mind. But what makes *Monumentum* unusual is not this image itself or its reference to the same gesture in *Les Sylphides*, but its inexplicable origin within the context of the ballet. In this way *Monumentum* is reminiscent of *Serenade*, a ballet with no story yet hints of narrative. The most extended of them in *Monumentum* is in the third part, when the two principals lose each other among a seeming throng who slowly crisscross the stage. When they do find each other, their reunion constitutes another of the ballet's sublime moments. She walks toward him and falls forward into his arms. He revolves her body and then wafts her upward again into a *développé*. The fall and recovery is so seamless, it takes your breath away. At a couple of points, Balanchine for some reason seems to have horses on his mind. All of a sudden the ballerina nods her head up and down. I suppose it's the long length of her neck supporting these bobs that establishes the equine association. It returns more forcefully in the closing passage, when the women buck their legs up high against their chests. (In current performances the reference is often lost, because the women do a conventional turned-in *passé* instead.) My favorite moment shows how a tiny detail can be transformative. The ballerina walks forward with her wrists twirling in the air. She makes a second pass and is joined by the ensemble, and instead of twirling their hands, she and her companions softly brush fingertips with their neighbors. In a flash, a purely ornamental gesture becomes human. In a flash, a feeling of fellowship. In a flash, it's gone. As is the entire ballet.

Liebeslieder Walzer

1960

Liebeslieder Walzer must be Balanchine's most beloved ballet, because in no other does he reveal as fully his love of women and his understanding of love's vicissitudes. I imagine Henry James enticed by its sharp eye for human relations, then transforming the ballet into prose. This is one way of saying how acute I think the ballet is.

The scenario is simple yet resonant. It is in two parts, the first to Brahms' Liebeslieder, Op. 52, and the second to his Neue Liebeslieder, Op. 65. In the first part the four couples who make up the cast waltz, in ballroom attire, in a drawing room large enough to accommodate the four singers and two pianists who play the music. The women wear long satin gowns and low-heeled slippers, and waltzing is what they do. In the second part the women wear tulle dresses and pointe shoes, and the waltz step gives way to classical dancing, with Balanchine deploying the full resources of classical technique. Asked by Bernard Taper (for his biography of the choreographer) about the marked difference between the two sections, Balanchine replied, "In the first act, it's the real people that are dancing. In the second act, it's their souls." Perhaps he was thinking of the vision scenes of many nineteenth-century ballets, in which the locale changes from, say, a village square to a place beyond ordinary experience, inhabited by sylphs and spirits. The transition from real to unreal in *Liebeslieder* is certainly in the tradition of the old theatrical convention, except that in *Liebeslieder* the transition has no great consequence; no one dies or is redeemed. The end of the ballet finds the four couples dressed again in their ballroom costumes, politely applauding the singers and pianists after they finish the last song. Yet much has happened within the last fifty minutes or so, and it is all enclosed within the convention of clapping your hands. This concluding return to society's rules is heartbreaking, but what would you have them do? Fly away forever in a sleigh, like Marie and her prince in Balanchine's version of *The Nutcracker*? That would contradict the tenor of the Brahms ballet, which, for all its rapturous dancing, is sad.

In part one the four couples waltz, waltz, and waltz some more. Always revolving, they turn inward, in *en dedans* circles. That is, they tend to move counter to the natural, forward line of direction. When the women turn under their partners' arms, they also move inside out, against the natural impetus or flow of the movement. As a result, we see the dancers' bodies in a somewhat shaded light, and moving with an energy resistant to the joyousness of *en dehors*, or outward momentum.

The accent of the waltz step is down; the women dip deeply on the first count. That first *plié* gives them a lot of upward spring to make the second and third counts sprightly, sometimes gay. But it's that initial downward swoop, into the floor, that sets the tone of melancholy. Indeed, its impact is so lingering that it influences what we feel about the rebounding second and third beats. Sometimes the dancers seem to be showing gaiety in the face of sadness. How resilient they are—and how noble, too.

This strong accent into the floor has dissipated since *Liebeslieder* premiered in November 1960, but it is still there if only in a ghostly way. It is emphatically present in the film I used to spur my memory of the ballet. Recorded in 1961 for Canadian television, it stars all of the original dancers with the exception of Melissa Hayden, whose role is taken by Patricia McBride. They are Violette Verdy and Nicholas Magallanes, Jillana and Conrad Ludlow, Diana Adams and Bill Carter, and McBride and Jonathan Watts. It is important for the reader to know my visual source for this ballet in particular. Part one is the most intimate dance Balanchine ever choreographed—it is basically a series of conversations—and all of the details that bring the intimacy to life are best caught by the dancers for whom he created the piece. First casts are almost always the best, but

Nicholas Magallanes and Violette Verdy in *Liebeslieder Walzer*. New York City Ballet. Choreography by George Balanchine © The George Balanchine Trust. Photo by © Martha Swope.

in this case the importance of gesture and timing over the steps themselves make the process of watching Balanchine demonstrate in rehearsal crucial. So closely are the original dancers linked with their roles that I have always found myself, fifty years later, identifying current dancers as the Verdy character, the Jillana character, the Adams character, and the Hayden/McBride character. So this is how I shall refer to them now. The men's characters are less defined. It's the women who carry *Liebeslieder*, and of them Verdy is the leader. I confess that everything I feel about the ballet has Verdy behind it. The critic Robert Garis, a great admirer of the ballet and of Verdy, wrote that although we follow the stories of all the women, it's Verdy we really track. I don't think this is absolutely so, but if it is, it's not because of the choreography.

The nobility in *Liebeslieder*, the transcendence over that first downward beat, is a quality that was a specialty of Verdy. You can see it in all the photographs of her in this ballet, and it also fully flowered later in the *Emeralds* section of *Jewels*. It's in her face—the downward cast of her eyes and the upward thrust of her chin. Take courage! her face says, knowing all the while that happy endings are not in sight. In *Liebeslieder*, the nobility of her strength is deepened by a knowledge that she, of all Balanchine ballerinas, is best able to convey: that the Brahms songs fill you with sorrow, and nostalgia. Verdy expresses these feelings with a slight rubato after every third beat of the waltz. It's an extra twinge of regret that her lingering pause gives.

Verdy's pause is musical, but there are many gestural pauses in the ballet as well. Sometimes the couples pause in mid-breath. What comes next? the Jillana figure asks just after her partner has her walking on air. He runs to her side as if to rescue her, and places his arm around her back, swinging her body into a turn. She receives his arm with gratitude. The Verdy figure wanders away from her partner, and when he comes to her side she receives his company with reserve. (Theirs is the most troubled relationship.) The McBride figure begins one of her duets in a dream state; she barely notices that her partner pushes her forward. She comes to her senses by boldly swinging her arms in a circle. Then she folds backward into a deep swoon. (There is much swooning in the first part; the Verdy figure even faints.) Many of the duets end with the man and woman embracing, or with the man kissing the woman's hands. Yet there is a pause before these resolutions. "How do I feel about this kiss?" the women sometimes seem to be pondering. The Verdy figure feels it as a temporary gesture. The Jillana figure gently walks toward her kneeling partner and peers over him with maternal solicitude, the line of her neck unbearably tender. The Adams figure mostly rejoices in her partner's embrace; indeed, she is the most joyous of the women, at least in the first part.

These pauses give a life-like texture to the dances. They are "real" people, as Balanchine says. They also create a sense of the thing not said, a kind of suppressed feeling very much like the end of the ballet, when the dancers simply clap for the musicians seated at the side of the stage. There are also happy moments in part one—a series of three trios almost

Patricia McBride and Bart Cook in *Liebeslieder Walzer*. New York City Ballet. Choreography by George Balanchine © The George Balanchine Trust. Photo © by Costas.

giddy in their playfulness and coquetry; a series of party games where the women sway back and forth toward each other as they sit on chairs all lined up in a row; or when all the couples link arms and dance in a circle. Interestingly, these ideas don't just materialize out of the unseen hand of the choreographer. One or two dancers nod or whisper to each other, as if to say, "let's do this figure now." The illusion that it's the dancers, not Balanchine, who are calling the shots gives part one its aspect of spontaneity, of life-like energy. My own favorite nod comes from the hips of two waltzing women, when they tip their hips toward the stationary women, inviting them to join in.

There's not one second in part one that is devoid of dramatic incident. Mostly you catch them on the wing; the only cautionary note to this reading is the danger of seeing glances and hesitations that aren't really there. But that's the nature of the beast. Yet there are two sustained events that stand out for their clarity and for the range of love experience they show. The happy one is for the Adams figure, when she strolls (in waltz time) across the stage while her partner whispers in her ear. In the 1961 film Adams cushions her neck against her whispering partner, as if reveling luxuriously in sable. How delicious it is to be adored! At the end of their meandering walk she herself becomes sable in her partner's hands. He lowers her to the floor and slowly revolves her in a full circle, savoring her weight and fullness of complicity. At the other end of the spectrum of human relations is one of the Verdy duets. Taking her partner by the arm, she leads him across the stage and then bends low underneath him, turning her body in full circle so as to expose her neck and bosom completely to his gaze. He responds by looking away from her, his hand shielding his face from her as they waltz. Do these moments chart a seduction rejected, and do they reconcile at the duet's closing? At the end she watches him embrace her back with his arms, but we don't know what her watchfulness means. She seems to be in a state of suspension as they slowly return to their seats.

One day the dancer Heather Watts and I were talking about *Liebeslieder*, in which she was then performing. We talked about the inclination to regard the women as people, something which makes the ballet unique in the Balanchine repertory. Suddenly, with a mischievous smile in her eyes, she asked me what role I would like to dance. No one, let alone a dancer, had ever asked me, a writer, such a question—outlandish, enchanting, seductive. I murmured, "The Verdy role." "Because it's the biggest part?" Watts asked. "No," I said, "because she's the person I'd most like to be: valiant, wise, and complex."

The Verdy part is indeed the biggest in the ballet. But how that role figures in each of its two sections tells you something about the nature of each. Part one is the more nuanced dramatically, the one with the most stories to tell. Balanchine gave the majority of them to her for the telling, because she was the most dramatically accomplished dancer he had. Part two is more about the act of dancing. You see it from the first moment of the first song, when the four women step onto pointe in big arabesques and then fill even more space when their partners lift them into the air. The fact that they have exchanged Karinska's long, heavy gowns for shorter tulle skirts obviously makes their bodies more visible.

Likewise, Balanchine has traded the first part's ballroom waltz step for a classical vocabulary, which means there is more to see from him as well. Part two is dominated less by the characters than by the two sections that have the most extended passages of dance. Instead of conversations, we have pas de deux. Instead of happy and sad dances, we have contrasts in allegro and adagio techniques. These exist in part one, but Balanchine gives them bigger play in part two, with outbursts of fast *piqué* turns and slow, deep arabesques.

The first major duet is for the Adams dancer. It spans three songs and is replete with supported adagio, two solos, and an allegro coda. It has one supremely exquisite moment, when Adams bends against her partner's back and is carried backward clear across the stage; once again, we are in the land of swoons. The duet can tell more stories as well, but it depends on who the narrator is. In the 1961 film, Gloria Govrin substituted for Adams in part two, and the upshot is a less rich pas de deux. Suzanne Farrell, dancing the Adams part years later, makes much of the dance a cry for freedom; at the end she more or less flees from her partner into the wings. But the main impact of this duet comes from its length and the fullness with which the dancer's technique is revealed. It happens that sitting above my desk is a photograph of Farrell and Sean Lavery at the concluding moment of her solo. Lavery clasps her wrists with a kiss, and Farrell's head turns sideways from him. The expression on her face is full of regret for not being able to accept his homage, and her shoulders are pulled up slightly, resisting the force with which he holds her hands. But what rivets my eye is not the emotion in her body but the gorgeous line of her foot pointed forward in *tendu*. I think that much of the beauty in part two resides in the play between feeling and technique. If, as Balanchine said, part two is about the soul, then Farrell's soul is in that arched foot, revealed in pointe shoes with the completeness that cannot be achieved in ballroom slippers.

The second major duet is for the McBride dancer, and it too has solos for the man and woman and an allegro section. Perhaps the most luscious moment in the whole ballet is in this dance. It is a pure dance image, devoid of any of the gestures and stances that enrich the earlier section. The magic moment occurs when the man lowers the woman as she unfurls her front leg forward and extends it so that only her foot and lower leg emerge from underneath the layers of her dress. Her partner helps her rise and dips her again. Slowly advancing in dips and rises, she repeats the passage three times, and each time her leg peeps out and retreats, it becomes more and more of a precious secret. In later years McBride refined the moment when her leg slides from underneath her dress by looking at her emerging foot rather than gazing straight ahead. By directing the audience's gaze toward her foot, she made the moment even more delicate, more exquisite. It's a moment when the choreography and the dancer's technical power to extend the leg with complete control and full turnout speak in one breath.

Liebeslieder Walzer is one of those ballets you can't see often enough, although there have been times when you haven't been able to see it at all. It played regularly during the 1960s, but in 1974 went into hibernation for the next decade. The official reason is that Balanchine felt that only first-rate singers would do justice to his dancers, and singers were expensive. The cost of singers was also a reason why the City Ballet did not produce *Liebeslieder* earlier. As early as 1951 Morton Baum, the virtual managing director of City Center and an amateur pianist as well, had been urging Balanchine to take up the music. It was put on the back burner through the 1950s. The unofficial reason for the hiatus in the 70s? Suffice it to say that *Liebeslieder* requires just the right cast. In 1984, a year after Balanchine's death, the City Ballet revived it at the New York State Theater. It had new decor by David Mitchell, which was grander than the original set by David Hays, designed for the smaller City Center stage. The many different casts who have been assigned the ballet since 1984 treat it respectfully, knowing that it is one of the great ones.

Raymonda Variations

1961

Strolling past the flower shops in my neighborhood on a fine spring morning, in search of a bouquet to bring home, I reject the bunches of lilacs and pink peonies. Impossibly pretty, I say to myself. Then I think of *Raymonda Variations* and realize how perverse is my reaction to the bouquets. For there is nothing lovelier than *Raymonda*, and if the peonies and lilacs elicit an association to the ballet, all the better. I buy the flowers.

In fact, *Raymonda Variations* is not pink and lilac but pink and blue—fluffy pink tutus for the women, baby blue for the ballerina, and a slightly paler blue for her cavalier. Flowers notwithstanding, pink and blue is not the most sophisticated color scheme for contemporary audiences. But then *Raymonda Variations* defies contemporary taste. It is a deliberate recreation of time long past, which in ballet time means the age of Petipa. Set to a score by Alexander Glazounov, it is one of many ballets described as Balanchine's tribute to his heritage. His Tchaikovsky ballets are equated with the Imperial age, because of their grandeur and brilliant virtuosity. *Raymonda Variations* is softer—it is meaningful that the women wear flowers in their hair instead of tiaras—and in the case of this ballet it is his heritage in a literal sense. As a boy he danced a small part in the Maryinsky's *Raymonda*, a full-length work choreographed by Petipa in 1898. Balanchine's treatment of *Harlequinade*, to music by Drigo, would also fall into this category, as would his general concept of *The Nutcracker*. (He danced the hoop variation in the original production, and by all accounts this is the choreography he used for his own production.) To my mind, though, most of his oeuvre is "in the style of Petipa." That is, the dances proceed from the academic language that Balanchine learned in school and Petipa used in his ballets. They show, at the very least, deference to the ballerina; at the most, idealization. And both choreographers share an ethos of courteousness, at the very least—romance, at the most—between the ballerina and her cavalier. Thus to say that *Raymonda Variations* captures the spirit of Petipa doesn't distinguish it from countless other ballets. Yet the Glazounov work does have its own fragrance.

Originally titled *Valses et Variations* when it premiered in 1961, *Raymonda Variations*, as it was renamed two years later, is just that. It opens with a waltz for an ensemble of twelve women, followed by a pas de deux and nine variations. A finale brings the ballet to a festive conclusion. Its structure is unusually simple; the variations are all solos, no quartets or trios. Musically, Balanchine pretty much lets Glazounov's melodies constitute the dancing's delight. He holds back from offering counter-rhythms, from making the texture of the choreography more complex than the score warrants. The one major exception is at the end of the ballerina's second variation, the ballet's ninth. She flies across the stage in a series of *pas de chats*, two to one side and one to the other, and so on. Although the music is in four beats, her phrases are in three. Splicing the four-beat measures into blocks of three gives all the *pas de chats* the gift of surprise and heady excitement, because she seems to be ahead of the music. Of course, it all works out neatly at the end. Four times three equals three times four. But that's it for musical games. What you hear is what you see.

The opening waltz is leisurely, even languid. Balanchine lets the ensemble move just as unhurriedly, with soft waltz steps, slow, broad *développés*, and luxuriously expansive arabesques and jumps. Of course, some of the foot work is faster, especially when the group moves into new formations, but the feeling of this waltz is that there's all the time in the world. Because of its gracious tempo and Balanchine's refusal to spice it up, this dance anticipates the opening waltz in *Diamonds* (1967). The one place where Glazounov introduces sparkle Balanchine marks with the entrance

Nina Ananiashvili and Andris Liepa in *Raymonda Variations*. New York City Ballet. Choreography by George Balanchine © The George Balanchine Trust. Photo © by Costas.

of the ballerina. It's a delicious entrance. Moving in a long diagonal, she flies in tiny *bourrées* past a line of pink tutus nestled on the ground, like the border of a garden. Pretty soon she's gone, and when she shortly reappears she forms the centerpiece of a picturesque tableau. What a lovely image with which to begin the pas de deux.

No matter how standard a pas de deux—the one in *Raymonda* is surely that—Balanchine always finds a movement that is out of the ordinary, and which becomes a signature of the dance. Here, it is a strikingly streamlined way of holding the body. The ballerina steps into arabesque with her arms pressed forward together, straight and with wrists crossing. Then Balanchine intensifies the image by having her fall forward into her partner's arms while both her arms and legs press together. And in the final moment of the ballet, she plunges into her partner's arms in a fish dive, but instead of one leg being bent in a *coupé*, both legs are straight as arrows. So here is a fish dive where the ballerina really looks like a fish (or a mermaid). When I conjure *Raymonda Variations* in my mind, I immediately think of the ballerina's long line from head to foot, and how different the look is from the rest of the ballet. There's a similar iconographic moment in *La Source*, to Delibes, in which the ballerina is carried across the stage with her legs pressed together, except that they are held in front of her body. In both ballets, the streamlined shape of the body injects a sliver of the twentieth century into very nineteenth-century ballets.

The nine variations look like they could have been made by Petipa, and that is their charm. (Indeed, the beginning of the man's second solo does duplicate Petipa's choreography for *Raymonda*, except that he made it for a male quartet, which Balanchine included in his *Pas de Dix* of 1955.) Scattered throughout the variations are an unusual number of hops on pointe, which have a decidedly old-fashioned look. They recall what local dance schools used to call "toe dancing," and, going farther back, Giselle's variation in Act I of that ballet. Balanchine uses those hops in his *Harlequinade* as well, and even though I don't find them particularly graceful, I enjoy them as signals that he is deliberately working in a bygone time. Two of the variations are fast and feathery. They would naturally be for small, delicate women. The fifth variation, which features the harp, is stately, strong, and andante in tempo. It's suited for a dancer with good balance. Another variation, featuring the sound of the triangle, is whimsical. Just how distinct each variation is depends on the imagination of the dancer, but the foundation is all there in the steps and the music.

The background of the ninth variation, for the ballerina, is interesting because it shows how chance can influence the final shape of the choreography. Patricia Wilde, for whom Balanchine created the role, says, in a video of her coaching various parts of the ballet, that Balanchine had originally designed a different variation for her but that when he resumed work months later, both of them had forgotten what he had choreographed. So he simply started over. In this video, which is part of the Interpreters Archive produced by Nancy Reynolds and the Balanchine Foundation, Wilde says that the first version was better, but to my eyes

Megan Fairchild in the "Hungarian" variation of *Raymonda Variations.* New York City Ballet. Choreography by George Balanchine © The George Balanchine Trust. Photo © by Costas.

the one we see today is nifty too. Moving with her arms folded across her chest and then extending them toward the audience in low ports de bras, palms up, the ballerina gives a hint of Hungarian demi-character style. Wilde says in the coaching session that here was one case in which Balanchine was very specific about the placement of the arms. Although ethnic coloration was applied lightly, it renders this variation different from all the others.

As much as I enjoy the interplay between Petipa and Balanchine, especially in the variations, I confess to loving the most quintessentially Balanchine material in the ballet. This is the finale, which is rip-roaring, a spirit that Petipa, by temperament perhaps, wouldn't dare dream of. It begins with the ensemble tearing across the stage two by two in fetching syncopations with the music. The dazzle culminates when the ensemble splits into two groups that stampede towards each other in two diagonals in traveling arabesques and contrasting tight *soussus*, in which the legs snap together in fifth position. But this is not yet the finish line. At the very end, the ballerina runs toward her partner on a diagonal, as if to leap into his arms in a fish dive, but in midcourse veers toward the audience. Her partner is there to catch her before she winds up in the conductor's arms. And yes, her legs are pressed close behind her, bringing a motif of the ballet to a jubilant ending.

The music for the finale is rambunctious—spoil-sports would call it circusy—and I love the ease and pleasure with which Balanchine takes Glazounov up on his cue. Although the rest of the score sometimes makes me wish it were by Tchaikovsky, Balanchine was obviously very fond of the music Glazounov wrote. The score is one of those to which he returned several times. (Another, by another second-tier composer, Mikhail Glinka, is the score for *Valse Fantaisie*.)

Balanchine's history with *Raymonda* in the West began in 1946, when he and the ballerina Alexandra Danilova produced a full-length though somewhat abridged version for the Ballet Russe de Monte Carlo. The music for the Grand Pas Classique Hongrois, from Act III, formed the core of 1955's *Pas de Dix*. *Raymonda Variations* is pretty much culled from the first act of *Raymonda*. In 1973 Balanchine returned to the Hungarian divertissement and named the new work *Cortège Hongrois*.

These ballets were designed as vehicles for the ballerina. *Pas de Dix* was created as a showpiece for Maria Tallchief, whose innate glamour reached its peak in the famous solo variation. The memory of her sultry *bourrées* and the bravado with which she threw her head back in the demi-character attitudes still makes me tingle. The ballet seemed pointless when she did not dance it. *Cortège Hongrois* was made as a send-off for the retiring ballerina Melissa Hayden. After she was gone, this shapeless, overly long string of divertissements lost its raison d'etre. *Raymonda Variations* was created for Patricia Wilde, with Jacques d'Amboise as her cavalier. Rather than celebrate what one already knew about Wilde, this ballet expanded her range. Already famous as an allegro technician, Wilde was here promoted, as it were, to full-fledged ballerina via the ballet's long pas de deux and lyrical fourth variation. Wilde was not cast in *Liebeslieder Walzer*, made the year before, and sometimes I wonder if Balanchine was not making it up to her with *Raymonda Variations*. In any case, of his four Glazounov ballets, this is the one that has flourished. With its demanding and delightful roles not only for the ballerina but also for a number of soloists, it forms part of the heart of the New York City Ballet's repertory. Although not one of the masterpieces, it gives the City Ballet its identity as a classical company. It has no dramatic subtext, no complexity of design, and no great music lifting it upward. If someone asks me whether they'll like *Raymonda Variations*, I answer yes, with the caveat that first you have to like pretty ballet.

Bugaku

1963

As a subject for ballet, violence was not congenial to Balanchine's temperament, but it did find its way into some of his work. In the cases of *La Sonnambula*, *Orpheus*, and *Prodigal Son*, physical violence was necessitated by the libretto. Cruelty, always a more potent form of violence, emerges in parts of *Don Quixote* and *Ivesiana*. What's notable in *Don Quixote* is that it wasn't driven by plot but by something more personal, by Balanchine's own vision of the essence of the novel (it is definitely not comic); in the Ives work he intuited violence in the music. *Bugaku* is unusual for its expression of sexual violence. One naturally thinks of the climax of the central pas de deux, when the woman faces the audience absolutely dead-on with her legs in a split. The image is astounding for its frankness—she does not face the audience at a more modest three-quarter angle, as she does in *Agon*—but what makes the moment violent is the effort it takes to get into that split. She more or less forces her legs open while her partner holds her aloft. Indeed, the entire pas de deux depicts the couple grappling with the extreme acrobatic positions Balanchine has given them. None of it looks easy; much of it looks grotesque, and at a really good performance your own stomach knots up in sympathy, and horror, for the bride. Actually, we only surmise that she is a bride and her partner a groom because of the long, white, gauzy trains that billow from the couple's bodies, and also because of the grave ceremonial activities that precede the duet. Some have called the ballet a nuptial rite. Allegra Kent, for whom the female role was created, gets at the ballet's ambiguity when she says in Nancy Reynolds' *Repertory in Review*, "It's some kind of ritual that has to take place, like flying fish mating." The man and woman are led into the breeding ground by their attendants, are stripped of their trains, leaving the woman in a bikini and the man in a body stocking, and are left to their own devices. What ensues is rape, but not the conventional kind. In *Bugaku*, the woman is a complicit party to the mating, because, as Kent says, it is ordained, and they both emerge from it as inscrutable as they are for the entire ballet.

The title refers to the dance music used in the ancient court spectacles of the imperial court of Japan. I do not believe that Balanchine was particularly interested in or drawn to classical Japanese art forms. In Martin Duberman's biography of Lincoln Kirstein, he quotes a letter Robbins wrote to a friend about Balanchine's reaction to the Kabuki theater, which visited the United States in 1960, three years before he set to work on *Bugaku*. Robbins wrote, "He thinks they're just a lot of old men standing around." The genesis of *Bugaku* begins with Kirstein. In 1958 the New York City Ballet toured Japan for a month, as part of a five-month tour of the Far East, and Kirstein became enthralled—perhaps titillated—by the traditional arts of the country. After much wheeling and dealing he was able to bring Gagaku (the dancers and musicians of the imperial court) to the United States, and the troupe gave several performances at the City Center during the City Ballet's season there in 1959. Whether or not Balanchine was as indifferent to Gagaku as he was to the Kabuki is not known, but Kirstein's enthusiasm for everything Japanese prevailed, and in 1962 the company commissioned Toshiro Mayuzumi to compose a score Japanese in spirit but using Western instruments. *Bugaku* premiered in 1963 with Kent and Edward Villella in the leading roles.

The choreography, too, is Japanese in spirit, although, especially in the first scene, it resorts to stereotypical notions about Japanese movement. The women bow and curl inward and roll their head sideways in stock geisha attitudes. They insinuate themselves, and the wheezing glissandos of the orchestra reinforce their not-so-innocent innocence. The men are samurais. They move in deep, wide stances, which Villella described as a

Maria Kowroski in *Bugaku*. New York City Ballet. Choreography by George
Balanchine © The George Balanchine Trust. Photo © by Costas.

"strut." They face the world with one shoulder forward: read, aggressive.
If *Bugaku* were only about slippery and stolid movement, however, it
would not go far. But it is not so much about movement as it is about
tone, something intuited rather than seen. In Duberman's biography he
quotes Kirstein's description of Japanese martial arts: "the inherent violence of most of the sports was contained within elaborate ritual bows,
self-composure, and a series of breathtaking postures and movement."
Kirstein's words well describe the feeling Balanchine was after in his ballet, except that Balanchine in the pas de deux exposes the violence lying
underneath and makes it explicit.

The idea of containment is felt in the dancers' mute faces and deliberate way of moving, and in the formality, and sheer number, of the

women's bows. It is best conveyed, however, in the decor by David Hays, which was inspired by the decor for the Gagaku theater. The dance space is bounded by a square cloth laid out on the ground and by a raised ledge that runs along the perimeters of the cloth. Slender ropes rising skyward lend elegance to the setting, but it's the demarcated space that gives the ballet its hothouse atmosphere. The dancers enter and exit from behind the back ledge and descend onto the dance floor on three steps, which gives their comings and goings ceremonial flourish. (How useful stairs are for expressing ceremonial import, not only in Japanese dance but in Petipa as well.) The attendants come and go single-file many times during the ballet, and sometimes I think that these solemn parades across the back of the stage are the most beautiful moments of the ballet; certainly they invoke the importance of what will transpire.

But what will transpire? The first section holds us in anticipation. The ballet begins with a long musical introduction, starting very softly as the strings slip and slide up and down scales as if trying to find their footing. When the curtain rises, there are no dancers on stage. The music continues to find its way, and still no dancers in sight. The air is filled with suspense, and so it still is at the conclusion of the first part. For even though the dancers do appear—first the women, then the men, then the women joining them in duets, and finally the women alone again—their posing and bowing and strutting seem introductory, mute as to intent.

After a pause, the second part begins, with the music registering a new urgency. The two principals enter from opposite sides of the stage and, having shed tutu and tunic, wear new costumes partly concealed by long trains. He carries her in floating arabesques and then the attendants enter. They place silk screens before the lead couple and remove the trains, so that they are "naked." The couple inch toward each other in low, wide extensions—low and wide is Balanchine's metaphor for Japanese—and once they touch their duet begins. After it's over, each does a solo—a cooling off period? She runs to him on pointe and he embraces her knees. The attendants return and clothe the couple in their chiffon robes. Now everyone dances together in what might be construed as resolution. Often the men waft their partners' trains high into the air; these filmy fountains of material might be interpreted as celebration.

Allegra Kent and Edward Villella in *Bugaku*. New York City Ballet. Choreography by George Balanchine © The George Balanchine Trust. Photo, Jerome Robbins Dance Division, The New York Public Library for the Performing Arts, Astor, Lenox and Tilden Foundations.

Irony is not a staple of Balanchine's theater, but the quality of suppressed or contained emotion is, although it is present for varying reasons. Sometimes the sense of the unspoken arises out of Balanchine's notion of what aristocratic comportment is like. In his most profound manifestation of containment, the man and woman simply bow to each other after a beautiful pas de deux. These bittersweet endings acknowledge the temporal strictures in which dance operates. Music is a formal, artificial structure with so many minutes' duration. When it's over, you say thank you very much for this dance, and then you go on. I don't think Balanchine kept the lid on in *Bugaku* as powerfully as in, say, *Liebeslieder Walzer*, or the ending of the duet in *Concerto Barocco* or of the andante in

Divertimento No. 15. Yet the power *Bugaku* does have hinges on contained feeling. Kent said that she always danced it "with a face that shows no emotion. Basically, I avert my eyes. I participate, but my eyes and face are averted from the reality of what's happening." The distinguishing fact about *Bugaku* is that the thing underlying the courtly rituals is brutal. Although the Japanese-style movement is largely pastiche, the extreme contrast Balanchine develops between the outer and inner, between the bows and the rape, brings to mind certain interpretations of Japanese culture.

Brahms-Schoenberg Quartet

1966

Brahms-Schoenberg Quartet is a big ballet on two counts. It is cast for fifty-five dancers, topping *Symphony in C* by three. And Schoenberg's treatment, in 1937, of Brahms' first piano quartet in G Minor is an effulgent gathering of Brahms' heady lyricism and Schoenberg's rich orchestration. Some musicologists have called the piece Brahms' fifth symphony. As a rule, Balanchine shied away from a big German sound, and as a rule he knew what he was doing. But in 1966 he decided to plunge into the Brahms/Schoenberg anyway—Stravinsky's protégé, Robert Craft, recommended the score—and the results are very mixed.

Of the four movements, the first three are moody, humid. But the last movement, the rondo alla zingarese, is a raucous affair musically; sometimes I imagine I hear Bronx cheers screaming from the brass. As another example of the subjective nature of sensory perception, Lincoln Kirstein compared the rondo to the cataclysm of World War I. In fact, as the critic Mindy Aloff recounts in *Remembering Lincoln*, Kirstein saw the entire ballet as an encapsulation of the history of the Austrian-Hungarian Empire. Less given than Kirstein to pursue a grand idea, Balanchine set the rondo as a gypsy carnival with everyone bedecked in streaming ribbons. Suzanne Farrell, the original chief gypsy along with Jacques d'Amboise, said in her autobiography that the movement reminded her of her days as a super in *Carmen* in her hometown of Cincinnati. I don't know whether Farrell, in

Jacques d'Amboise and ensemble in the fourth movement, rondo alla zingarese, of *Brahms-Schoenberg Quartet*. New York City Ballet. Choreography by George Balanchine © The George Balanchine Trust. Photo © by Costas.

mischievous mode, was drawing a parallel between Balanchine's take on gypsydom and its conventional presentation in opera, but if so she was correct, for in spite of the witty faux-hauteur of her gypsy persona and the hijinks of d'Amboise, choreographically the section is hackneyed. There's simply too much strutting and skulking and head-tossing (read abandonment). And for all the exuberance of some of the dancing, it doesn't match the energy of the score. With music that reaches a crescendo every few minutes, you keep waiting for Balanchine to hear the call to arms and give us a whopping climax (or two) of his own. But it's not in the cards.

The section that best captures the music's moody atmosphere is the third, the andante. As a preamble to the music's stately unfolding of melody, the cast fills the dance space before the music starts, softly settling in to their opening formation as if it were a down pillow. We know where we are before the first note of music is heard. From there, it's slow-motion dancing. The ensemble sway their arms from side to side, like bowers made heavy with dew. The cavalier lifts his ballerina extremely slowly and promenades her for what seems an eternity. It's not, actually; it's just that the dancers are taking their time, giving full measure to the ripeness of the music. That ripeness is most beautifully expressed when the ensemble falls into two lines and forms a necklace of intertwined arms, one line kneeling and the other bending over them, then bending backward. Wearing Karinska's gorgeous full skirts of pink tulle, the dancers are like a garden of roses just after a rain. Meanwhile, there are undertones of restlessness in the music, which Balanchine brings to the fore with the three demisoloists quickly circling the flower bed in double time (a tactic he uses in the intermezzo as well, and with the same effect). There is also a sprightly martial melody interjected into the atmosphere, which evolves into a dashing solo for the man. His solo is, in truth, a welcome relief from the languor of the rest, but it's that image of the luscious lines of women that stays most vividly in the mind.

Because the andante so firmly positions the audience in the ambiance of the music, I wish that Balanchine had decided to open the ballet with it. It would not have been the first time that he switched the order of movements, which he did most memorably in *Serenade.* But he took the conventional route and began the ballet at the beginning of the score. And that's the movement that presents Balanchine with a musical problem he doesn't solve. This might not be worth dwelling on, were it not so rare. For it joins a mere handful of Balanchine works in which music and dance don't see eye to eye. For example, the nervous edge of Stravinsky's *Card Game* and *Danses Concertantes* (the second version, for the Stravinsky Festival of 1972) eluded him. The first couple of songs for *Who Cares?* turn Gershwin's wit into show-biz cliché. A couple of jazz scores choreographed in the early 1960s left him high and dry, perhaps because at heart he had no sympathy for American jazz.

At issue, I think, in this first movement of *Brahms-Schoenberg* is tempo. The score is marked "allegro." Yet as the way the New York City Ballet orchestra plays it, and as two recordings I have of the piece also play

The ensemble in the third movement, andante, of *Brahms-Schoenberg Quartet*. New York City Ballet. Choreography by George Balanchine © The George Balanchine Trust. Photo © by Costas.

it, the tempo wavers between allegro and andante. Moreover, the dark coloration of Schoenberg's orchestration accentuates the slower over the quicker. Balanchine choreographs this movement as if hearing in his mind the feeling of the third, andante part, but arranging steps that are more suitable to an allegro tempo. Dancing allegro steps at the slow pace the City Ballet orchestra gives to the music presents practical problems. Jumps, for example, are in allegro territory; how do you jump slowly into the air? How do you sustain a normally allegro dance phrase over a long period of time? One of the major dance themes of the section, taken by the soloist, goes like this: big traveling jump, followed by two steps on the floor, followed by a big pose in arabesque. To fill out the time, those two steps on the floor have as much emphasis as the jump and pose. Usually, Balanchine favors a contrast between large and transitional movements. With each part of the phrase given equal weight, the effect is not so much somber or grand as heavy. In phrases that include a big *grand jeté*, the woman obviously cannot linger in the air at andante speed; so she bides her time with a slow *glissade*, another transitional movement. And another ponderous dynamic. The problem of moving slowly without the aid of a partner also arises in the later, truly andante movement. But here Balanchine gives the women many ports de bras, which don't need assistance from men. And the principal woman has a partner to help her negotiate the slow tempo.

Besides tempo, the first movement has another problem as well. The music alternates between two themes, and Balanchine acknowledges the changes with, I believe, unwise obedience. As a result the choreography is overloaded with entrances and exits for the principal couple, the female soloist, and the ensemble. There are no extended passages of dance. Was Balanchine seeking a sense of agitation, which certainly informs the music? Perhaps, but to me the comings and goings offer a quite different scenario: Balanchine chasing after the music. The one moment where he wraps his arms around the score is at the very end. As the music turns its darkest color, the dancing slowly, slowly winds down. The principal couple walks gravely in a circle, their outstretched arms forming a space through which the ensemble passes. Gently, the ensemble find their places and kneel while the lead woman continues her circling, alone. To the last strains of music the four men evaporate into the wings. It all feels like a farewell, the one instance where the dancing has emotive substance. Just before the men depart, the male principal lifts his partner onto his shoulder. It's the only false move in this denouement, because the shoulder lift has too much brio for the sad mood Balanchine has established. Still, this long farewell is the one passage I can visualize in my mind when I listen to the music by itself. One of my private pleasures is to listen to music at home and visualize the dancing that goes with it. Tellingly of the helter-skelter feel of the first movement, the two-for-one trick doesn't work.

Melissa Hayden, for whom the ballerina part in the first movement was created, describes the problem from a personal perspective, in Nancy Reynolds' *Repertory in Review*. She says, "It was one of the few things Balanchine ever created for me in which I did not feel comfortable. He started out with fantastic steps that required very intricate partnering, which he could do but others could not. It was going to be like the best of *Liebeslieder* on pointe, very difficult, but it had to be watered down and watered down. I lost my identity in it."

Patricia McBride, in the first cast of the second, intermezzo section, also reports trouble in *Repertory in Review*, but her story has a happy ending. She says, "He started it, but seemed to be having problems, practically the only time. He took a few days off, went away. When he came back, it went so fast; he finished the movement in about an hour. It was as though everything had formulated itself in his head while he was away, then just melted into place. One step flowed into another. It's such a beautiful thing, very difficult with timing. But the partner does it all. I'm off-balance all the time, mostly bending back. I actually have a special arc for Brahms."

The critic Arlene Croce noted an unusual flexibility in McBride's lower back, which perhaps makes possible the special arc McBride refers to. In any case, you see that arc right away, when the ballerina thrusts her front leg way forward in a low lift, then presses her foot deeply into the floor while her upper body swoons backward. In another kind of configuration, she bends way back and is also dipped toward the floor at a tilt. Or is it the floor that has tilted? Which is to say, while the couple is dancing the world seems daringly askew, intoxicated, intoxicating. When Kirstein described the ballet as a world "drunk on wine and roses," he must have been thinking of the intermezzo. And when a performance is especially on target, the audience, too, feels woozy.

Supporting the duet's embodiment of high romanticism are the fleeting exits and entrances of three women, whose runs and whirls in double time with the music bring out its inner pulse of unease. And, of course, the fact that these hovering presences number three gives them a touch of portentousness. The duet passages are some of the most alluring Balanchine has done, and in their concentrated pursuit of off-balance movement they are tours de force. There is a tendency, however, to focus exclusively on Balanchine's pas de deux at the expense of the corps, especially in a duet as powerful as this one. The importance of the three whirling women in giving the whole section a feeling of danger can't be underestimated.

Coppélia

1974

Along with *Swan Lake*, *Harlequinade*, and *The Nutcracker*, *Coppélia* is one of four nineteenth-century-based ballets that Balanchine admitted into the New York City Ballet repertory. Traditionally, *Coppélia* is played as a comedy. The story is about Swanilda and Frantz, two young lovers whose romance goes awry when Swanilda spies Frantz blowing kisses to a beautiful young woman who sits on a balcony overlooking the town square, reading a book. What they don't realize is that the woman is a doll, created by Dr. Coppélius, typically played as the village eccentric. At night Swanilda steals into Coppélius' workshop, where she eventually learns the truth about the woman on the balcony. In Act II Frantz breaks into the workshop as well but encounters Dr. Coppélius. He tells the old man that he loves the woman, whereupon Dr. Coppélius conceives of his grand dream. He will drug Frantz and transfer his life forces to the doll, bringing her to life. Meanwhile, Swanilda has dressed herself in the doll's clothes and deceives the doctor into believing that the doll is indeed a breathing woman. After creating havoc in the old man's quarters—she turns out to be a rambunctious young lady—she shows the lifeless doll to Coppélius and Frantz, who has finally awakened from his slumber. The victorious Swanilda runs off with Frantz, leaving the heartbroken Coppélius alone with this heap of lifeless limbs. In the third and final act, celebrating the town's new bells, Coppélius runs on stage with his ruined doll and is given a handful of money. He runs off, angrily shaking the money in his hands, as if a few coins could make amends for the collapse of his experiment. That's the last we see of him. There follows then the proper business of a happy ballet, which is a series of divertissements concluding with the a nuptial pas de deux for the bride, Swanilda, and groom, Frantz, and a joyous finale.

What makes the New York City Ballet production of *Coppélia* different from others is that it counterpoises the story's comedic line with the tragic story of Dr. Coppélius. He was performed originally by Shaun O'Brien, who, under the direction of Balanchine and a former wonderful Swanilda, Alexandra Danilova, created a character larger and darker than the standard portrayal. He is not a funny old geezer. (Balanchine cautioned O'Brien not to play him as too old a man.) Thus when the town boys harass him and rough him up, he fights them off with physical spirit and a sense of moral outrage. They are ruffians; he is a gentleman. But it's the way he sets about drawing from Frantz the life forces (what else to call it?) from his eyes, legs, and heart and giving them to the doll that sets up the tragedy. As mimed by O'Brien and a few subsequent dancers as well, we understand that his scheme is almost Faustian in its ambition. (A punster, Balanchine in rehearsal called the book that Coppélius studies for guidance the *dybbuk*, referring to a ballet Jerome Robbins had recently made on a similar theme, the pursuit of the forbidden.) Every move that Coppélius makes, whether turning the pages of that black-magic book or placing his cupped hands over the doll's breast to make it breathe, is riddled with trembling energy. Dare I do it? he seems to ask with avidity and fear. Conveying the momentous nature of his endeavor, his arm movements seem to emanate from the pit of his stomach and reach toward the sky. The timing of his gestures elongates the rhythm of the music, giving gravity to the task he has set for himself. It's just as well that Swanilda disabuses him of his dream, because, after all, his wish to invest with life a mechanical object goes against nature. But the poignancy of his realization that he has been tricked is not forgotten—at least, not entirely.

When Edwin Denby, in the collection of his reviews *Looking at the Dance*, wrote about the Ballet Russe de Monte Carlo's performance of *Coppélia* in 1944, starring Danilova, he tellingly makes no reference to

Patricia McBride as Swanilda, Shaun O'Brien as Dr. Coppélius, and Mikhail Baryshnikov as Frantz in Act II of *Coppélia*. New York City Ballet. Choreography by George Balanchine and Alexandra Danilova, after Marius Petipa (1884) © The George Balanchine Trust. Photo © by Costas.

Dr. Coppélius, whereas the reviews of the City Ballet production dwelled on him. For Denby, the narrative interest of the ballet "is the serious good sense with which it treats a serious subject—the basis for a good marriage." The idea of a good marriage is located in the pas de deux of the two lovers at the end of the ballet. Denby writes, "When you see their motions and physical proportions beautifully balanced, when you see them harmoniously overcoming impossible difficulties, you have seen a convincing image of what would make two lovers happy in marriage. . . . On the other hand, the pitfalls that prevent marriage are told in the earlier action, when the boy is infatuated by a beautifully mechanical doll; he wants a real girl and he wants an ideal one in addition. In this psychological dilemma, like a man, he goes to sleep. But the girl, like a Shavian heroine, solves the dilemma by her independent courage. And then the boy proves his real worth by his strength and his gentle control in the nuptial dance duet."

Denby saw in the pas de deux form a metaphor for love, but I think the metaphor is overstretched in *Coppélia*. Indeed, I have heard many women say that, the duet notwithstanding, they can't understand how such a bright young woman as Swanilda could ever go for a dumbbell like Frantz. As for their harmony, Balanchine made a wry commentary on that matter when in the coda he had his hero and heroine jumping up and down in opposing counts, like the sparring lovers in a screwball comedy. Yet Denby hits the nail on the head when he describes the passive nature of the hero and the aggression of the heroine, which encompasses courage, of course, but also the almost manic energy of Swanilda, at least as she was played by the City Ballet's first Swanilda, Patricia McBride.

The first thing she does as a pretend doll is hurl to the floor the little red book we saw the doll holding in Act I. That action is in the choreography, but the enthusiasm with which McBride flung the book has yet to be matched. In contrast, the real doll, sitting on the balcony, moves her book in exact time with Delibes' plunks of music, which wittily imitate the mechanical movements of a doll. Swanilda's humorous, and fierce, rebuttal of book-learning is just the first crank of the gears toward mayhem. By the time she's finished, she has Coppélius on his knees in befuddlement and alarm. Be careful what you wish for, he must be thinking as he mops his brow. You might wish Swanilda were a little less energetic when she goes on a tear, were it not for her understandable desire to rouse Frantz from his stupor. She does, and she triumphs at the moment when Coppélius collapses in grief. Just in case you do not realize that the ballet belongs to Swanilda, and not to Coppélius, in Act III she claims as her own the most triumphant passage of music in the whole score. She dances it as a solo.

Coppélia got off to a rocky start. It premiered at the Paris Opera in May 1870, on the eve of the Franco-Prussian war. The music was by Delibes and the choreography by Arthur Saint-Leon, with a libretto by him and Charles Nuitter. It was based on the story "Der Sandmann" by E.T.A. Hoffmann, which provides the foundation for the dark tones in the City Ballet version. The opera house soon closed because of the war; another victim was *Coppélia*'s star, the talented sixteen-year-old Giuseppina Bozzacchi, who died of pneumonia within days of the premiere. Although the ballet continued to be performed in Paris after the war, it was Petipa's new production in 1884 that put it on the international map. Balanchine and Danilova knew it from their student days in St. Petersburg, and it was more or less the version that Danilova danced with the Ballet Russe de Monte Carlo, beginning in 1938 in London. For the New York City Ballet's *Coppélia*, which premiered in 1974, Danilova staged the first two acts and Balanchine staged the third act plus the two character dances in Act I and Frantz's solos in Acts I and III. He made the solos of necessity, with music borrowed from other Delibes ballets, because Frantz in the first production was danced *en travesti*. Thus, there was no music for a proper male variation.

Obviously, Balanchine was on hand to refine everything. During rehearsals I remember him adding little touches to the "ear of wheat" duet for Swanilda and Frantz so as to make more vivid her disenchantment with him. The long passage of classical dancing for Swanilda and her friends he left as is—it is a delicious example of Petipa's art—although he did embellish Swanilda's solo with a few extra steps, to thicken the stew. The rehearsals—at least, the few I was lucky enough to attend—seemed to be happy times. As Danilova's students at the School of American Ballet knew, she adored dancing full out whenever she got the chance, but the opportunity to be partnered by Balanchine was something else! I cherish the memory of her and Balanchine running through the ear of wheat duet and Danilova's determination to hold her balances for as long as possible. Balanchine was amused: once a ballerina, always a ballerina.

Just as Balanchine brought the ear of wheat pas de deux closer to what Swanilda was feeling, so did he bring the two character dances in Act I closer to the world in which the lovers live, a town in the area of Galicia in eastern Europe. The mazurka and czardas, the two mainstays of national dancing in the Russian classics, are by convention danced by the upper class. They are elegant, and for *Cortège Hongrois*, which Balanchine made in 1973, he left them that way. For *Coppélia*, however, he made the dances folksy. The mazurka looks like a polka; it is boisterous, full of bounce. The czardas looks like no other national dance I, for one, have ever seen. Its signature movements are big *battements*, and instead of circles we have straight lines. Balanchine said that the dance is from the Carpathian mountains. Perhaps it is because I am so accustomed to the

Joaquin De Luz as Frantz in Act III of *Coppélia*. New York City Ballet. Choreography by George Balanchine and Alexandra Danilova, after Marius Petipa (1884) © The George Balanchine Trust. Photo © by Costas.

czardas of *Raymonda* and *Swan Lake* that this Carpathian dance always startles me. Yet despite the novelty of the czardas and the gaiety of the mazurka, they are too long. (Balanchine chose to use all the repeats in the music.) Feeling time drag in a Balanchine production is the biggest surprise of all. I still wonder why he didn't shorten these dances. I also wonder why they interested him in the first place, since national dances are usually low man on the totem pole, especially as they are performed today. One explanation for Balanchine's interest could be that character dancing was and is still esteemed in Russia. In fact, the one dancer who was always singled out above all in Russian commentaries on *Coppélia* was Alfred Bekefi, who led the mazurka and the czardas in St. Petersburg until the end of the nineteenth century. He brought the house down.

Coppélia premiered during the City Ballet's annual summer season in Saratoga Springs in upstate New York. Balanchine had long fretted about the company's ability to fill the large outdoor theater. This resort town's audience was less urbane than the one in New York City (Balanchine called it "the masses"). But he had a "popular entertainment" plan up his sleeve—to include in the ballet many children, who would bring their siblings and parents to the theater. Using children as bait also informed his conception of *The Nutcracker*, but the truth is that he used student dancers as often as possible. He himself had performed in many ballets during his school days, and the marvelous memory of the experiences stuck. For *Coppélia* he used twenty-four tiny ones, and although their choreography is simple, they form the backbone of the entire third act. They introduce the first of the variations, the Waltz of the Golden Hours, and then frame the Dawn, Prayer, and Work (or Spinner) variations, as well as a quartet of Jesterettes. The invention and charm with which Balanchine uses them as background is incomparable. Sometimes he groups the lot of them in picture-postcard formations, and sometimes he arranges them in small groups, some dancing in bouncy *pas de basques* while others scurry to other places on the stage. Sometimes only their arms move to accompany the soloists. To greet Prayer they seat themselves on the floor, complementing the calm of her dance. Their activities are always in perfect balance with the soloists' work, and they make the stage bloom.

Indeed, I sometimes think that without the children's presence the solos would look thin; on the other hand, Balanchine created these solos with choral amplification in mind. Taken by themselves, the solos are pleasant. Of special interest is the dance of the Jesterettes, because it is an example of Balanchine introducing a bit of black and white austerity into a Technicolor world. In contrast to the other divertissements, this one has tight footwork and is relatively static, its energy springing from the dancers moving on consecutive beats. It's a deliberate attempt to lower the prettiness factor, just as the Marzipan dance does in *The Nutcracker*.

The one divertissement intended to make you smile is the one called Discord and War. After the Jesterette dance, the sky darkens and the children run off. To blaring horns, on gallop a group of Valkyries in full regalia. To understand where on earth these warriors come from, you need only listen to the music, which ribs Wagnerian bombast. I like the joke in principle but not in fact—the choreography's vigor is strained—and I am always happy when peace returns and the bridal couple dance their lovely duet and jubilant solos.

Fans of Balanchine enjoy turning his repertory into a parlor game. What's his best ballet? Ensemble dance? Finale? In the last category the one in *Coppélia* is a close second to *Symphony in C*. Balanchine's finales are games in themselves, the goal being to build a maze and end up in a clearing. The one for *Coppélia* works like a precision machine. Although the entire cast is whooshing by in a panoply of pattern, dancer A's left shoulder is always there as a guidepost for dancer B's right shoulder. Snaking lines collaborate neatly with straight lines. And, somehow or other, a giant merry-go-round that threatens to jam breaks into a semi-circle just in time for a higher echelon of dancers to pace one another in galloping turns. Yet the activity is comprehensible to the eye. Each category of dancer, from the friends of Swanilda to the bridal couple, is introduced separately before they are jumbled together, and even then a pecking order is maintained. The steps are fast and furious, naturally, but they cluster around one family of movement whose nucleus is the prancing *emboîté*. Finally, it is possible to anticipate the dancers' paths of movement in one eyeful. It is possible, that is, until the end, when Balanchine springs a surprise on us. Usually, climactic moments file by singly; here, we have a double one. When Swanilda dashes along a hedgerow of village friends and makes a running dive into Frantz's arms, you figure this is the pinnacle. Not so. At the very instant of Frantz's catch in the near-left corner of the stage, all the children and the soloist from the Waltz of the Golden Hours bound on from the diagonally opposite corner, as though shot from a cannon. And this entrance is only the launching pad for another thrill. En masse, the kids and their leader make a beeline for Frantz and Swanilda and seem to be headed for an awful collision, the machine gone haywire, when suddenly they U-turn and head toward their niche at stage right. And that takes us right into the clearing, a short spell of unison dancing with hero and heroine at stage center.

Balanchine was in a playful mood when he devised the *Coppélia* finale. He decided to build the structure and have everyone run through it in one fell swoop, without testing it for flaws in timing, spatial relationships, and possible hazards for the dancers. The thing worked, and the dancers applauded. Another kind of pleasure took hold of some of the older dancers, as they remarked to each other that this finale was another version of the one for *Harlequinade*. They took gratification in identifying the family resemblances among the repertory, one reason being, I think, that it made them feel part of the Balanchine family. Happily for this audience member, he did not choreograph the entrance of the children at the rehearsal I saw, and so I was able to gasp with first-time surprise at their entrance during the premiere.

Le Tombeau de Couperin

1975

Le Tombeau de Couperin was created for the Ravel Festival of May 1975, and in any circumstances its loveliness would have been welcome. In the context of the Ravel Festival, however, it was a welcome relief. To this day this ballet seems the sole justification for the three-week endeavor, at which sixteen premieres were presented, eight of them by Balanchine. The Stravinsky Festival of 1972 produced plenty of duds, but unlike in that festival, Balanchine failed to lift this one by dint of his own work. A couple of his new pieces were stale. A few others were vehicles for star dancers, though only Farrell in *Tzigane* returned the favor in full.

Why Ravel? was the query surrounding the festival even before it got under way, and the skepticism behind the question was supported by Balanchine's own history with the composer. It was scant. There were only *La Valse* and two early attempts at capturing the delicate poetry of *L'Enfant et les Sortilèges* in his portfolio (his third try, for this festival, didn't get at the heart of the music or libretto, but one could surmise at least that he was attached to the score). Surely he would have done more with Ravel had he been more attracted to him.

Because Balanchine had used Stravinsky many times before the Stravinsky Festival, the composer's style of music had become a kind of lingua franca within the company. All the choreographers who set ballets for the tribute had at least a modicum of experience with the music and an idea

115

of what to do with it. Ravel was unfamiliar territory, and many of the ballets they created were without footing. So why all of a sudden should Balanchine and his co-choreographers—Jerome Robbins, John Taras, and Jacques d'Amboise—devote so much effort to giving Ravel the kind of exploration and celebration the company had given to Stravinsky three years earlier, or for that matter to Tchaikovsky in the festival devoted to him in 1981? The question goes unanswered, although Barbara Horgan, Balanchine's personal assistant at the time, conjectures that he chose Ravel because he thought the music danceable, appealing to the general public, and something the other choreographers could handle.

There are no lingering questions about *Le Tombeau de Couperin*. It's about as perfectly constructed a ballet as Balanchine ever made. The music pays homage to both the eighteenth-century composer François Couperin and to friends of Ravel who died in the Great War. The ballet pays homage to squares, circles, and straight lines, and to all the visual ramifications therein. It is perhaps Balanchine's most conceptually oriented work and to my mind a stunning example of how the form and meaning of a dance can speak to us in one voice. It is also a daring departure from his usual format, in that instead of being set for an ensemble and principals, it has an ensemble only. The cast of eight couples is divided into two quadrilles, which remain politely yet firmly discrete until the middle of the third dance. Balanchine calls the two groups quadrilles because their choreography is inspired by social dances. The first of the four sections, the Prelude, is the one that most closely adheres to the genre. It is done in the square formation typical of barn dancing, and anyone who has ever spent an evening square dancing would have no trouble calling out the figures—ladies' and men's chains, four-hand stars, promenades—or recognizing the etiquette unique to the form—the endless curtsies and little sashays acknowledging three categories of neighbors: one's partner, one's right-hand couple, and the group at large. The women dance on demi-pointe. Gradually, the technique grows more elaborate. By the second movement the women move on full pointe, and two of the motifs are arabesques and *grands battements*. But it's not until the third section that the ladies take to the air.

The core formation of the second dance, the Forlane, is two lines of eight, each shaped into a gentle V. Much of the dancing is done in diagonal lines, so as to reshape what could be a harshly horizontal field of action into a merry carousel of angles. Besides creating spatial interest, Balanchine inserts a musical story as well. The groups move forward and back on consecutive phrases, so that each quadrille is divvied up into the left and right hand of a piano score. (The music was originally composed for piano between 1914 and 1917, and Ravel orchestrated it in 1919.) The steps of the third and fourth dances, the Menuet and Rigaudon, are enlarged versions of the first, but here the reel predominates. And in the third dance our entire field of vision changes, for instead of occupying the left- and right-hand sides of the stage, the two quadrilles are for a while located at the front and back of the stage. The relationship between the two groups looks less friendly, though there is certainly no suggestion of opposition.

How Balanchine arranges the groupings so that each has a different weight and feel, and how he arranges the multitude of promenades and ladies' chains so as to make each unique are as much a part of the ballet's story as are the dancers' exquisite manners and ambiance of graciousness and high spirits, especially in the last dance. *Tombeau* poses and answers questions relating to the very core of formal values, and there's no getting away from them. The ballet compels you to notice that the first dance would look flatter and feel heavier were the squares not sometimes tilted into diamonds and softened into circles; or that in the second and third dances the difference between parallel and intersecting diagonals is the difference between the public and the domestic. You marvel at Balanchine's ability to juggle between the two without snagging the ballet's fleet pace. Similarly, you must notice the delicate balance between vernacular and classical language. The gentlemen's hearty handshakes in the final movement would be a breach of idiom were they not immediately returned to the fold by the women's little hops in attitude *en avant*. You begin to see also that bent legs are cozy and content; straight legs are for getting somewhere else. Bent legs belong to *Tombeau* in its circular, domestic mood; straight legs to the linear, more public side.

The ensemble in the fourth movement, Rigaudon, of *Le Tombeau de Couperin*. New York City Ballet. Choreography by George Balanchine © The George Balanchine Trust. Photo © by Costas.

You notice all these things, if only on a subconscious level, because Balanchine presents them transparently, persistently, and rationally. You could diagram it, perhaps computerize it. Many of his ballets define their boundaries and rules of play as they are being played out at the time of performance, but in *Tombeau* he presents them to us as a prearranged story. There is one plot line, however, that emerges as the ballet moves forward, and it's the one that makes the ballet's formal and dramatic lines fuse: when will the two quadrilles become one? The issue is not pressed; it may not even arise for some viewers. But the question kept me on the edge of my seat. The unification happens in the third dance, when the men exchange partners across the divide, on the other side of the hemisphere. Because this happens almost in tandem with the ballet's first big lifts, the ballet suddenly pops into full bloom. Then he enlarges the great coming-together. Everyone joins into a star formation. And finally, for just a moment or so, the whole notion of pattern is abandoned altogether.

The group splits into couples, who saunter about casually. Mon dieu! It could be a moment out of Robbins' *Dances at a Gathering*.

In the last dance Balanchine departs from another of the ballet's precepts. *Tombeau* has been an ensemble piece. Now comes a passage of solo dancing. After a prelude of jolly heel-and-toe rusticity, the group lines up for a reel. Perhaps taking as a cue Ravel's charming solo passage for a clarinet, Balanchine sends the lady at the head of the reel down the center of the two lines, while everyone else kneels. She walks daintily on pointe, yet there is a piquant sting to each of her steps, perhaps because they match the music note for note. The deliciousness of her little journey is rationale enough for setting the ballet on pointe rather than on what would be more authentic footwear, slippers. (The fact that the original lady was Judith Fugate, who was endowed with spectacularly arched feet, added extra spice to the moment.) It's still one of my favorite moments, and so are the ones that follow. After the woman reaches the end of the

Judith Fugate and Laurence Matthews in the fourth movement, Rigaudon, of *Le Tombeau de Couperin*. New York City Ballet. Choreography by George Balanchine © The George Balanchine Trust. Photo © by Costas.

line she is met by a man who rises to escort her in a little circle. Then another couple steps into the limelight and they are soon joined by a woman. The transition from couple to threesome and back to coupleness passes without a ruffle. Three is no crowd; three is just three. A few more solo and duet turns transpire before the music catapults the group out of the reel formation into another shape. But those few minutes when a few from the anonymous line claim their place as individuals have always enchanted me. I find myself asking a question that forgets the basic reality of any dance, that it is choreographed. How is each solo dancer appointed? How does she or he know when to get up and sit down? The feel of these moments is not one of improvisation. One intuits governing rules; who rises and who stays seated seem to be preordained. Yet there is no governor in sight. What we have is a self-governing society, a utopia. Starting with Edwin Denby, many critics have noted that Balanchine's ballets are metaphors for civility. In *Le Tombeau de Couperin* Balanchine takes good behavior to a new height.

Chaconne

1976

Were I not leery of absolutes, I would declare the opening pas de deux of *Chaconne* the most haunting one in the Balanchine canon. If it has a competitor, it would be the "walking" duet of *Emeralds*, the one Balanchine made for Mimi Paul. The *Chaconne* ballerina was Suzanne Farrell, and what distinguishes both dancers, besides their beauty, is the permanent imprint they left on their respective roles. The duets are different in that the one from *Emeralds* never recovered its mysteriousness after Paul left the New York City Ballet. *Chaconne* has fared much better, perhaps because Farrell was around much longer than Paul, leaving ample time for her influence to seep into the minds and bodies of her successors. Today, when we watch the parts of *Chaconne* created for Farrell—the opening duet, of course, and the minuet and gavotte that come later in the ballet—the dancer before us reveals Farrell as her guide and as a memory more or less vivid, depending on performance. (The performance Farrell gave for the television program "Dance in America" shows her, alas, as a dim reflection of her own self.) Thus in writing about the Farrell parts of the ballet I encounter a tension between choreographic facts and the images they evoke. Am I responding to what is inherent in the steps or to my memory of the way they were done? Ah, it's the proverbial dancer versus dance conundrum. This is always the case in writing about an old dance, but with *Chaconne* it's just more so. When I write about the power of a leg at a certain moment, I describe in part the power that Farrell gave to it.

These ruminations were occasioned by rereading a review of *Chaconne* I had written just after its premiere, in January 1976. I've decided to use much of the Farrell-related part of that review in this volume because it captures the ballet at its richest. But reader, beware! What you read here isn't always what you get from your seat in the audience today. On the other hand, much of the review does apply now, because, as has been said a thousand times over, the expressive power of the steps transcends all—most of the time.

In a prelude to the duet, an ensemble of women mournfully walk about the stage in lovely patterns, accompanied by Gluck's "Dance of the Blessed Spirits," from the opera *Orpheus and Eurydice*. As they depart, a man and woman slowly walk toward each other from opposite sides of the stage. Her eyes are cast down; his focus is on her. After a meditative pause, their bodies revolve around each other and their arms intertwine. They make each other's acquaintance with the calm measure of foreknowledge; that's why these two figures strike me as godly. Their embraces are more inquiring than Gluck's serene flute music, but not until the woman embarks on traveling lifts and walks does the tension between aura and data develop into drama. As the flutes amble about the Elysian Fields, the woman's powerful, long legs compel the man to skim her through what seems to be the universe. Those long, low strides are grandly calm, befitting gods in their element, but they are not accomplished without will—her will. Everything about her presses forward. Like a real swan, without flutter and self-caressing fuss, her bottom leg tucks up beneath her lifted body and surges forward in acknowledged power. Her toe nips the ground, her wrists and neck press lightly down, and she's off again. Despite Gluck's heavenly music, the ground is part of her world; indeed, parts of her journey are totally terrestrial. With her partner mooring her, she leans away from him and etches circles on the floor with the narrow tips of her shoes. This circular route from here to there is not the most economical, but the care with which she works her feet renders this journey the most exquisite. Nor does the ballerina avoid treacherous routes. She leans back into her partner's arms so that she is almost parallel to the floor, cranes her head backward, and with her partner as guide carefully extends one taut leg in front of the other.

Balanchine has a particular fondness for these not-so-enchanted walks in the enchanted garden. As in ballets like *Baiser de la Fée*, *Emeralds*, and *Stravinsky Violin Concerto*, the one here seems to intimate that the dancers' effortless grace is hard won and precious, that heaven is entered through a gate. By showing us in *Chaconne* the underside of the serene lifts and dancers' demeanor, he darkens and enriches the flute music. In this duet Balanchine again discovers the point midway between the stratosphere and the empyrean. When the woman propels herself and her partner across the stage and into the wings, you imagine them pressing onward for the rest of time.

Who are these dancers and where are they dancing? Presumably they are Orpheus and Eurydice reunited, even though the "Dance of the Blessed Spirits" takes place in the Elysian Fields, where Orpheus has not yet reclaimed his beloved. It's not wise, though, to tie Balanchine to a literal rendering of the opera's libretto, particularly this one, which ends with a conventional happy ending. He would be much more in tune with the story he worked out with Stravinsky for their ballet *Orpheus*, which ends with the deification of the artist. There is another mythic story, however, that the duet conjures with its swimming imagery, the music's elegiac calm, and most of all the sense of eternal motion suggested by its ending. Possibly, these two lovers are Odette driving Siegfried through Tchaikovsky's waters, calm after the storm.

And that's that for the otherworld. The lights brighten and a small ensemble walks on stage and forms a semi-circle. They stand at attention, the flute gives way to full orchestra (from the last act of the opera), and the four couples cross the stage in stately arabesques. At once we are in a different climate, and the shock of the transition continues to reverberate even after the curtain falls—even though the ballet's gorgeous dancing offers plenty of distraction, to say the least. In *Chaconne* Balanchine once again illustrates how the ABC's of academic vocabulary can be manipulated into visions of grandeur. Following the ensemble's traveling arabesques, Balanchine brings on the entrées of the rest of the cast: the demi-soloists and then the groups who will perform separate variations. He

The New York City Ballet in *Chaconne*. Choreography by George Balanchine © The George Balanchine Trust. Photo © by Costas.

slides each group into the frame seamlessly, so that the canvas stretches, stretches, and stretches some more, almost imperceptibly. Not until the entire cast poses in a tableau do you fully realize how far Balanchine has taken us—from a few modest arabesques and ladies' chains to a design of splendor. Whereas the opening duet was drenched in feeling, this grand entrée is pure white-on-white. If pressed to identify its setting, you might say it takes place in court, were court and stage not synonymous in Balanchine's ballets.

The following variations are as translucent. Banking on the inherent strength of academic steps, Balanchine shows us how baby talk may be eased into singing, supple sentences. Avoiding a didactic simplicity, he drops dabs of color into the dances without subverting their whiteness. In the pas de trois, the man carries his arms as though they held a lute; sometimes he plucks imaginary strings. His two ladies swish their skirts as though they were fancy dresses. (In fact, they wear fairly simple skirts.) In the following duet, the dancers remind one of court jesters with the broken lines of their arms. Whereas the trio is gracious and relaxed, the duet darts and spins. Next comes a crisp, adorable pas de cinq for kittens—at least, that's what comes to mind when the lead dancer curls her front leg in, snuggling it against her back leg. Finally, the couple who danced the opening duet returns in more elaborate costumes for a duet and variations. Now *Chaconne* tilts into more vibrant colors, but in the context of the preceding dances, with their small coloristic signatures, the two stars do not carry the ballet away with them. Rather, they lace essentially four-square choreography with coloratura shape and dynamics. The woman hops and bounces through evenly spaced footwork, but it's the circular route her body makes from A to B and her speed that make these passages high voltage. You'd never recognize her simple *soutenu* turns for all the scoops and spirals she embellishes them with. Especially with Farrell dancing, the *soutenus* make her the Joan Sutherland of ballet. The man also has some dazzling moments, like the dead stops in second position, but his choreography is more even-keeled. Separately, they tat contrasting fabrics; the man, especially when he was Peter Martins, irons out the material while the woman, especially Farrell, crinkles hers. The complementary nature of their solos precludes competitiveness, but the moment that makes the heart soar is given to the man. Throughout the variations, the man and woman spell each other at obvious transitions in the music. At one transition, however, the man keeps going. It happens when Gluck ratchets the music up a notch, and the man responds to the musical surge with a corresponding second wind in his muscles. As for me, I levitate.

The ballet concludes with a chaconne, which, along with the rest of the music in what can only be called the ballet's Act II, comes from the last act of Gluck's opera. To divide the ballet into two acts speaks to the peculiarity of *Chaconne*. Were it perfect, there would be a link between the opening ensemble dance and duet and the rest of the ballet. Unity of tone has never been on Balanchine's must-do list; nevertheless, the contrast between parts one and two is hard to swallow. You might say that *Chaconne* is a magnificent ballet with a magnificent flaw. Arlene Croce also found the ballet's contrasting parts disconcerting, but she attributed it to the introduction of rococo style for Farrell. In *The New Yorker* she wrote, "what happens in the middle of *Chaconne* is that a whole new ballet crystallizes, a new style of rococo dancing appears. . . . The first pas de deux gave no hint of what was to come." Nancy Reynolds, in *Repertory*

Suzanne Farrell and Peter Martins in *Chaconne*. New York City Ballet. Choreography by George Balanchine © The George Balanchine Trust. Photo © by Costas.

in Review, feels that the work's discrepancies may result from its having been created over a period of years. She also notes that the dances were originally created as interludes between parts of the opera and not meant to be seen one after the other.

The basis of the New York City Ballet *Chaconne* was a full production of the opera given by the Hamburg State Opera in 1963, for which Balanchine composed all the dances. A decade later it was brought to the Paris Opera, where Balanchine made some revisions. Yet another version was performed by the Chicago Lyric Opera in 1975. The most famous, or infamous, Gluck/Balanchine partnership was in 1936. Although a veritable newcomer to the United States, Balanchine, much to his delight, found himself installed as the resident choreographer of the august Metropolitan Opera in New York. He, Lincoln Kirstein, and the painter Pavel Tchelitchev conceived of an *Orfeo* so radical in concept and design that it is hard to imagine it being allowed to proceed beyond the first rehearsal. First and last of all, the singers were in the pit. Although it had only two performances, it became a crucible around which literary intellectuals and the conservative press squared off. Partly because of the controversy it sparked, the production has become part of the lore surrounding Balanchine's early adventures in his adopted country, and the fact that it is lost only adds to its legendary place in the Balanchine/Kirstein annals. Kirstein wrote at length about it, focusing mainly on Tchelitchev's contribution, which was probably more central to the production than Balanchine's. Ruthanna Boris, a dancer in the production, provides a telling if fragmentary description in *Repertory in Review* of what the dancing was actually like: ". . . slow walking, bending . . . a kind of organic movement growing out of what was happening—as though people were talking to each other. This has nothing to do with pantomime—but it's relating—body language. Actually, it was full of those marvelous encounters that happen all through Balanchine's works, which nobody pays any attention to—*Liebeslieder*, *Serenade*—there's no story, but people are always transacting something together."

Remnants of the opera's style show up in the Stravinsky/Balanchine *Orpheus* of 1948, in the importance given to decor (Noguchi) and lighting (Jean Rosenthal), and also in the organic nature of much of the choreography. Counting the Stravinsky *Orpheus*, *Chaconne* is the sixth time Balanchine returned to the Orpheus legend, although its story is tangential to the City Ballet *Chaconne*, if it's there at all. The material to which he kept returning is Gluck's music.

Union Jack

1976

A ballet in three parts, *Union Jack* begins in the ether of the Scottish highlands, then plummets to the streets of lower-class London. The third part is neither as high as the opening tattoo nor as low as the Cockney pas de deux. This concluding hornpipe belongs to no class or place. It's just pure joy. When I first saw *Union Jack*, at a gala preview in May 1976, I tried to sew the three pieces together by finding cross-referencing commentary. The only thing this critical exercise accomplished was to exercise my imagination, leaving the ballet itself in tatters. *Union Jack* is what you see, and that is plenty. At least, it's pretty much what you see. The first chapter of part one, the tattoo, carries a feeling and evokes emotions beyond its marching steps.

The first part is some forty minutes long, of which the opening tattoo is about nine. (At the first performance it was a good deal longer. Balanchine said he knew it was too long but wanted to see it anyway. By the second performance he had excised a few minutes. I don't remember if I thought the long version was unduly so; what I do know is that I still wish that the tattoo would continue for as long as the dancers, all seventy of them, hold out.) The tattoo is divided into seven regiments. After a separate entry for each, they march en masse. There follows a recessional, after which they return clan by clan for a spell of Scottish dancing. Then all the regiments join together, in couples, and leave Scotland far behind. To the hymn "Amazing Grace," the men support the women in large arabesques and *grands développés à la seconde*, and all of a sudden we could be in the Maryinsky theater watching a Petipa ballet. Done en masse, these tableaux are emblems of classical ballet, and the parallel Balanchine draws between kilt and tutu signals the importance of the tattoo.

In the tattoo each regiment parades under the arches of Rouben Ter-Arutunian's whimsically designed bridge toward the front of the stage. It halts for four drum beats, marches in a maneuver, halts again for four beats, and parades to the side of the stage. As one regiment is moving to the side, the next is already entering under the bridge. Dressed in tartans, the marchers' galaxy of blues, reds, greens, yellow, black, and white swell the stage in great waves. The momentum is incredibly compelling, the colors glorious, and the number of personnel thrilling to behold. But the heart-stopper moments are those four-beat halts. For reasons that remain inexplicable to me, they tilt the extravaganza into something austere, perhaps a bit archaic. They mark an event outside of one's experience, and the dancers' observance of it gives them nobility. This is especially so when the dancers stop time with one arm raised high in a curve. Here we are, those raised arms proclaim, and so shall we be. Later on, during the Scottish dances, you notice that the raised arms of the tattoo are similar to the raised arms of the jigs, but slightly different, more classically rounded. These small differences puncturing the effect of mass movement are another reason why the tattoo section is fascinating. The men and women do the same steps, yet differently. The men's tread is heavier, more somber. Wearing pointe shoes, the women extend their front feet in embryonic *battements tendus*. Imitating the drag step in British military parades, the dancers' back legs pause a second before moving forward. The women add to that pause a slight, slight intake of breath, giving their walk more spring than the men's. The four-beat freezes come in different varieties. Sometimes the arms rise, sometimes not. On occasion the pose is in profile. And the women in the final regiment, the Royal Canadian Air Force, break protocol by tossing their heads backward as they raise their arms. (This contingent will be even naughtier when they are reincarnated as WRENS in the hornpipe section.)

The New York City Ballet performing the opening tattoo of *Union Jack.*
Choreography by George Balanchine © The George Balanchine Trust.
Photo © by Costas.

These tiny differences show Balanchine working with a microscope, and noting them provides an excitement akin to the pleasures of watching Lucinda Childs' and Laura Dean's minimalist 1970s pieces, made contemporaneously with *Union Jack*. But of course it's the grand scale of the tattoo that takes your breath away. The logistics of maneuvering this seventy-person corps de ballet into ever-changing formations made Lincoln Kirstein compare Balanchine to a general mapping out his battle plans. I myself think of Petipa sitting down at his chess board, as the story goes, arranging the chess pieces as he might wish to see them on the Maryinsky stage. The craftsmanship with which Balanchine arranged his troops was a given long before this ballet. But the twining and breaking apart and twining again of the tattoo artists is something else! Shortly before the premiere of *Union Jack* I interviewed Balanchine prior to a rehearsal. Not his usual chatty self, he asked me if he could end the interview early, because he needed time to prepare for the rehearsal. He needed to figure out a way to get everyone off the stage, quickly. "It's not so easy," he explained. No, indeed.

Just as Balanchine introduced high ballet, in the "Amazing Grace" passage, into the high ritual of the tattoo, so might he have continued the train of thought by incorporating ballet into the following divertissement of Scottish folk dances. But he didn't. The five Scottish dances that comprise the bulk of part one are what they are—jigs, which are as close to their source as the tattoo is to its source. The bobbing and crisscrossing of legs is lively enough, but not as powerful as what came before. Both sections trade on repetition; the difference is that repetition in the tattoo is hypnotic, whereas in the jigs it presses down on you. Much of the problem is musical. As orchestrated by Hershy Kay, each of the songs seems a reprise of the former one. It doesn't matter that Balanchine gives each dance a distinctive format; the music takes one back to square one each time. Sometimes Kay gets fancy: in the third dance, for a male and female regiment, or clan, the simple tune spins into a fugue and then gathers in a Broadway-sounding conclusion. But this stab at musical embroidery runs counter to Balanchine's determination to keep the jigging pure. It is not surprising that the one winner in the divertissement is done to drums only. The ten ladies of the MacDonald of Sleat clan gallop on like wild stallions, unbound by anything but the four-beat rhythm of their march. Their legs lash out in furious kicks; their arms heave up and forward, so that their jackets threaten to come off. You could say that this dance is a rebuttal of the tattoo, were it not for the fact that the women never stray from the beat. The dance brings the house down, and I bet that every woman in the audience sends personal greetings to these fierce creatures who dance the pants off everyone else.

From the splendors of Scotland we now descend into Costermonger land, where the Pearly King and Queen entertain us with a pas de deux. He carries a red rose and a handkerchief for her use when she feels rebuffed; she carries a flask. Set to Kay's orchestrations of vaudeville songs, the section is most convincing when Balanchine sticks to tried and true vaudeville routines, like a soft-shoe turn for the gentleman and his umbrella. Sometimes, though, the tried and true seems tired. Thus the jokes about scene-stealing remind you of the same jokes in older Balanchine ballets, such as *Bourrée Fantasque* and *Donizetti Variations*. Those jokes weren't so hot either. One-liners and Balanchine are not best friends; his humor is best when it grows out of a musical context.

The original Pearly Queen was Patricia McBride, and her consort was Jean-Pierre Bonnefoux. Here we had a Russian-born choreographer designing English music-hall paces for a Frenchman, with native-tongue results. This melting pot of culture became something of a tradition in the Costermonger duet, with Mikhail Baryshnikov and later the Danish-born Nilas Martins taking up the umbrella with ease and evident enjoyment. The sight of these "foreigners" unself-consciously adapting an English accent is the loveliest joke of all in the duet. And let us not forget the master impersonator behind it all, Balanchine, who plunged even farther into English culture in the concluding section of *Union Jack*, a homage to the Royal Navy via the hornpipe.

Balanchine lived and worked in London in the early 1930s, after the death of Diaghilev left him, and most of the ballet world, without a home. He made dances for several revues, but they were rather high-end. In his off-hours he must have ventured into the music-halls proper. He had also choreographed a couple of hornpipes in 1926 for the Diaghilev-produced *The Triumph of Neptune*, in which he also danced a solo role, in blackface,

Jean-Pierre Frohlich, Karin von Aroldingen, and Joseph Duell in the Royal Navy section of *Union Jack*. New York City Ballet. Choreography by George Balanchine © The George Balanchine Trust. Photo © by Costas.

of the drunken Snowball. The critics who saw the ballet wrote of the hornpipe dances with affection, and sometimes awe. When the New York City Ballet was close to premiering *Union Jack*, the company invited the Royal Ballet, which was dancing at the Metropolitan Opera, to watch a rehearsal. I watched this rehearsal as well. After the hornpipe section was finished the Royal's old timers stood up and cheered, some of them laughing and crying at once. They were simply incredulous that Balanchine had been able to get at the essence of the dance—its free-wheeling joy. "How does he know about this?" they exclaimed. "I haven't seen this since I was a boy!" How Balanchine knows about it is a rhetorical question, to which he once answered, "You look in the refrigerator and see what's inside."

The Royal Navy section opens with a "pas de trois," which I enclose in quotes because, even though it is set for three dancers, it is as far from the codified formality of such nomenclature as the entire navy section is from the tattoo. Three sailors come skipping on with arms freely swinging, and at once we're in the realm of blithe spirits. Later on, larger groups intermix with smaller ones in no particular order, or so it seems. What grabs you is the spontaneous feel of the whole thing. Sailors have work to do, of course, and so there is much sailor-business going on—throwing ropes out to sea and hauling them in, managing sometimes-rough waters, scanning the horizon through spyglasses—all conveyed in cartoon-like mime. But who are the sailors on the lookout for? When the WRENS (Women's Royal Naval Service), dressed in fetching white shorts, make their saucy hip-swaying entrance to the Colonel Bogey March, we get the answer: sailors of the opposite sex. The tattoo marcher who wore the most resplendent of the hats becomes the raunchiest of the sailors, with bulging muscles to boot. One piece of nonsense that I missed during the first years of performance is now a favorite: the sailors skip around the stage in the shape of a navy bean.

The hornpipes are an obvious parallel to the series of Scottish jigs in terms of the ballet's format, but the former enjoy a few advantages. Coming after the tattoo, the jigs have a tough act to follow, but the hornpipes burst upon the scene freshly born. Step-wise, the contrast between the sailors' skittering feet and rubbery legs offers a liveliness missing from the jigs. The biggest difference, though, is the musical accompaniment. The sailor ditties offer Kay more room in which to elaborate, have fun with. Sometimes I think it all comes down to music. Both the Scottish and Navy parts end with grand spectacle: the clans reassemble for "Amazing Grace," the sailors line up for "Rule, Britannia." Regardless of the way Balanchine arranges these homages, the Scottish one is bound to be more effective just because "Amazing Grace" is better music than "Rule, Britannia." Nevertheless, the way he does arrange the naval tribute is curious. The dancers pass each other banners, and when everyone is duly equipped, they semaphore "God Save the Queen" as a multi-layered Union Jack flag descends. This semaphoring brings to a screeching halt the rollicking pace of everything before; the dancers stand flat-footed as their arms signal a message you wouldn't understand unless you've read the footnote at the bottom of the program. (This is the only time in the whole of the City Ballet repertory when you've got to consult a program to know what's going on.) But at least the message isn't garbled, although this was not initially the case. Barbara Horgan remembers that her colleague Edward Bigelow, on the administrative staff, was dispatched to the main rehearsal room to teach the maritime ports de bras. Facing the dancers, he demonstrated the moves. Only when he got back to his office did he realize that he had taught the positions in the reverse direction. Back to the studio he went, this time facing the mirror, with his back to the group. So okay, God save the queen, in the right direction, and once that's done, bring back the hornpipes. But no. The curtain falls as muffled guns mutter a five-gun salute.

Union Jack was the City Ballet's offering for the United States bicentennial. It all makes humorously inverted sense until the end. Was Balanchine meaning to poke fun at patriotism? Or is the semaphoring a straightforward gesture gone flat? The Costermonger section strikes me as a miscalculation as well, a very long holding pattern to give the dancers time to change from kilts to sailor suits. The terrain *Union Jack* covers is vast, and the results are very uneven. Sometimes I rearrange the parts in my mind as if they were pieces of an imperfect jigsaw puzzle. What about starting with the hornpipes, then moving right into the Scottish dances, and saving the magnificent tattoo for last? As for the Costermonger entr'acte—well, I don't know what to do with it except toss it. But this is the critic in me writing. When at home, removed from the immediate impact of the ballet's imperfections and able to think about it as a total experience, I love the whole damn thing. The dancers have never looked more worthy of Balanchine's heritage than in their tartans, and never more adorable than in their sailor outfits. Today, when many of Balanchine's ballets are under-danced and devoid of meaning, *Union Jack* still measures up to Balanchine's intentions. The dancers make the case.

Vienna Waltzes

1977

Vienna Waltzes is set to five waltzes by three composers. In order of appearance, they are Johann Strauss' "Tales from the Vienna Woods" (1868), "Voices of Spring" (1885), and "Explosion Polka" (1848), followed by Franz Lehar's "Gold and Silver Waltz" (1905) and Richard Strauss's waltzes from his opera *Der Rosenkavalier* (newly arranged in 1944). Vienna between 1848 and 1944 underwent enormous political changes, ending in catastrophe. The decor by Rouben Ter-Arutunian depicts signature changes in decorative style only. His first set represents the gentle woods, dappled in light in front and misted in the back. Five trees stand in the dancing space. (This was Balanchine's idea, Ter-Arutunian said, and formed the scenic foundation for what was to follow.) After the third dance the trees rise, their roots becoming a kind of Art Deco gate. Beardsley-like drapery dabbed with red comes down to decorate the front of the stage. For the fifth and final dance, the stage is stripped to a vast silver ballroom, its dimensions made ambiguous by a mirrored back wall, which has been there all along but had been obscured by scenery. The roots of the trees have become ciliated chandeliers. Balanchine's scenario also suggests change: from country to city, flirtation to seduction, natural love to supernatural love, forest to movie studio.

Although it is tempting to view *Vienna Waltzes* through a sociological scrim, it is actually shaped by Balanchine's tried and true formula of the well-planned meal. The governing idea is variety and contrast. The challenge is to show that three-quarter time is interesting enough to sustain fifty minutes of dancing. More specifically, how do you make a satisfying meal out of sweets? For although Balanchine's ballets have always waltzed, in that they are lyrical, strongly rhythmical, and civilized, the combination of J. Strauss, Lehar, and R. Strauss is a good deal more caloric than Tchaikovsky. Balanchine meets both challenges head on, yet as a meal *Vienna Waltzes* does not satisfy completely, simply because not all of the courses are entirely tasty in themselves. As with *Union Jack*, though, the parts matter less than the whole. The utter gorgeousness of these waltzes and of the costumes Barbara Karinska designed for the dancers is superior both to today's pretensions of simplicity and to glamour on the cheap. *Vienna Waltzes* sweeps by in total conviction of that fact. It's better to be rich than bourgeois. It's better to be very big than just big, as the finale with seemingly hundreds of waltzing couples proclaims. The audience at the time of the ballet's premiere in 1977 thought so too. It was the most popular ballet the New York City Ballet had ever produced.

After a rousing overture from "Tales from the Vienna Woods," the curtain opens on a stage bare of people. We are given a moment to absorb place. To the strains of a zither, one couple strolls into the woods, their heads tilted toward one another in whispering reflection and tilted, too, in a studied manner so as to elongate the line of their necks. For all the intimacy of the zither's sound and the couple's posture, the woods is a public place, the love-walk a study in the art of the promenade. And sure enough, the privacy of their entrance quickly yields to a glittering panorama of waltzing couples as the zither yields to the full orchestra. The couples waltz and waltz some more around the trees, which from time to time become a vehicle for hide and seek. The men's heavily braided uniforms and the women's full pink dresses just grazing their ankles suggest a classy school prom, but the formality of their groupings and the sweet lilt of the waltz step suggest a cotillon. In this part, the purest exposition of the waltz, you focus on the changing patterns and the way Balanchine uses them to soften his strict adherence to the ballroom step. You notice that the difference between a waltz step with a free swing into the first beat and one with a pause after the second beat is the difference between daytime and nighttime romance, between sunny and clouded weather. "Tales from the Vienna Woods" has a touch of the latter, expressed by the lead couple. Their romance is a poignant *affaire*, in which her gently suppressed ardor suggests an older woman on the arm of a tenderly obliging youth. Will he come to her side after all the other men have joined their ladies? Ah, he does, but the few seconds when the woman stands alone, the confidence of her pose shaded by a sliver of vulnerability, embody all the tension rising out of the waltz's metrical hesitations. In the waltz, you never know all is well until the third beat.

From the ballroom waltz Balanchine moves to ballet waltzing. The female lead and an ensemble of eight women wear tulle; the man, tights and tunic. Their full-out classical dancing—this is the only section where pointe shoes appear—promises the richest development of waltz time even though nary a waltz step is used, but in fact the breezy jumps and turns around the trees turn out to be the thinnest material in the ballet. Balanchine's menu formula makes a classical section inevitable, but I have a feeling that his heart wasn't in it, that he was bowing to the principle of variety.

The surprise of a formulaic classical-ballet waltz comes back to back with another one: that a ballet dominated by the lushness and good manners of the Viennese ballroom should have as its mid-point anchor a rambunctious polka for dance-hall girls and pot-bellied dandies in coxcombs and striped suits. The beer hall invades the woods. Bobbing replaces gliding. Heads had nestled against shoulders; in this dance noses nuzzle against bellybuttons. Instead of pivoting the ladies around in circles, the men crawl between their ladies' accommodating legs. The explosion in the polka's title Balanchine arranges as a kind of bump and grind, which hurtles the men to their backsides. The interesting thing about this polka is that although the women's steps are bawdy, they move with refinement, almost delicacy. No matter what their class, Balanchine wants to keep the ladies properly feminine, in this ballet and all others. We may be put off by the men because they are so grotesquely dressed, but we take delight in the ladies' sauciness.

The fourth section takes us into La Belle Epoque, with the scenic transformation under way as the opening bars of Lehar's "Gold and Silver

Sara Leland and Bart Cook in the third movement, Explosion Polka, of *Vienna Waltzes*. New York City Ballet. Choreography by George Balanchine © The George Balanchine Trust. Photo © by Costas.

Waltz" are played. Now the waltz becomes ultra-suave. The women ease their way into the arms of their partners without so much as a bow. The invitation is understood by innuendo. The seduction of the man in red by the exquisitely dressed woman in black is also by innuendo. Nothing need be declared; everyone knows what they're there for. This is the ballet's erotic interlude, and Balanchine places the man and woman in the waltz's most erotic embrace. Always revolving around each other, the couple dance back to back, her arm stretched across his shoulder blades and her hand curled around the nape of his neck. The focus is on the couple: will they or won't they? Balanchine couldn't make up his mind. One version ended with the man and woman separating. In another, the man stood alone. In the final version, the couple stand closely together in silhouette. Maybe they repair to the boudoir. Maybe not. Balanchine keeps us guessing all the way through, which of course adds more erotic tension. The curious thing about this waltz, though, is that it doesn't sizzle as much as it's supposed to. I think this is because the ensemble is relatively static. Basically onlookers, they promenade about the room and barely dance, thus flattening the atmosphere.

The "Gold and Silver Waltz" is worldly, and the three preceding sections are of this world. In the concluding one, to waltzes from *Der Rosenkavalier*, the scenic transformation into an empty space takes us out of this world. Across the wide silver plains of this ballroom glide couples in black tuxedoes and svelte white satin gowns with long trains. Even from the vantage point of the front of the house's orchestra section, the stage is distant, remote. The moving figures appear as architectural models imposed on a tundra. Unexpectedly—for there is no obvious musical clue to her entrance—the "girl in white" emerges from the shadows. (I give her that name because she is singularly alone and perhaps doomed, like the girl in white in *La Valse*.) She floats to the center of the stage, and though her back is turned to us, the magnitude of her presence changes the tundra into a haunted ballroom. She lifts one arm, bows and rises, embraces the air, and waltzes free-form. She moves not on the beat, or off it. She is pure motion—gliding, swaying, breathing. Her arms languidly twine in the air like the tendrils of the trees' roots, now seen in the chandeliers, and fall back across her throat in unearthly caresses. Out of nowhere a gentleman joins her for a few turns. She lifts the train of her gown across her face while waltzing in his arms, but to assume that this gesture signifies a desire for privacy is presumptuous. This waltzer dances to her own, unfathomable tune. The man is a phantom, and she might be too. This perhaps imaginary partner joins her a few more times. Sometimes her back shudders and heaves in his arms. Surely she does this in response to the music's emphatic pulsations, and perhaps as an expression of grief, mourning. Who knows but that she is a prophet of disaster? (At the first couple of performances I imagined I heard, later on in the ballet, the muted sounds of guns in the slight tapping movements of the women's feet as they whirled in circles.) But back to what is "real" in this dream

Suzanne Farrell in the fifth movement, to music from *Der Rosenkavalier*, of *Vienna Waltzes*. New York City Ballet. Choreography by George Balanchine © The George Balanchine Trust. Photo © by Costas.

world. The couple's solitude is broken by a few minutes of waltzing by a phalanx of other couples—an interlude I have never understood—and when they all leave the woman continues her wanderings as if never interrupted. She exits in a deep backbend, and the chandeliers burst into bright light. The two actions happen simultaneously, so that you are not sure if it's her plunge into the wings that triggers the blaze of light, or vice versa. Some observers say that she immolates herself.

Her self-immolation, which I buy only if the dancer's backbend is sufficiently intense, ignites a stupendous finale comparable to a Hollywood spectacular. Their numbers doubled by reflections in the mirrors at the back of the stage, the entire cast waltzes, and the trains of the women's gowns waltz as well, as they fly in the air. Sometimes the patterns of the forty-odd couples are formal, but mostly there is no pattern. The entire spectacle coalesces and diffuses with seemingly random movement; the constant is the onward surge of the waltz. This is why the very final moment of the ballet is startling. Out of the maelstrom there is suddenly order. The five principal couples, who had been embedded in the crowd, end up in the front line, and all the women curtsy genteelly. We could be back in the Vienna woods.

Vienna Waltzes was the last of Balanchine's extravaganzas, coming just a year after *Union Jack*. Because these two ballets premiered in quick succession, one might want to lump them together, in retrospect, as a concerted last hurrah. But the ballets couldn't be more different. The waltz ballet places Balanchine in familiar territory. In format and content it's conventional stuff. *Union Jack* is radical in every way, beginning with the very premise of the ballet and going on to the daring exposition of the tattoo (nothing but marching!), and an unusually extended use of folk dance. The tattoo has a depth of feeling that *Vienna Waltzes* doesn't approach, and it springs from that part of Balanchine's sensibility that conjoins pageantry and religious devotion. Because of its solemnity and willingness to go on for as long as it takes, and possibly for longer than the audience wants, it most closely resembles, to my mind, the long processional of religious figures at the end of his *Don Quixote*.

Despite the differences between these two big ones, it is possible to sense in Balanchine a period of sustained exhilaration in the late seventies.

The dancers were on a high during these years as well. A revival of *The Four Temperaments* in 1976 was extraordinary for its vitality. The always-difficult *Divertimento No. 15*, with eight principals, had the luxury of two different casts. And then there was *Chaconne*, which after its premiere in 1976 grew ever more lustrous in performance. A dance-goer friend of mine who didn't believe in generalizations, especially if they were happy, was moved at the time to declare 1976–78 a golden period of the City Ballet.

Vienna Waltzes was the last ballet for which Karinska designed the costumes. She died six years after its premiere, in 1983, the same year as Balanchine. The ballet's success would not have been possible without her expertise and imagination. She made elegance and extravagance natural partners. With this gift of hers, she was Balanchine's soul mate throughout his entire American career.

Mozartiana

During the preparations for the 1981 version of *Mozartiana*, Balanchine and the costume designer Rouben Ter-Arutunian fussed a great deal over the coloration of Suzanne Farrell's tutu. The other dancers were dressed in black; Farrell's tutu would be white with a black overlay. The question was how black and how white would her tutu be? The shape of the tutu was also discussed. Would it be short (and perky) or knee-length, giving her body a weightier shape? Eventually, the longer tutu prevailed.

Balanchine made four earlier *Mozartiana*s, the first of them for Les Ballets 1933 and the last, in 1945, for the Ballet Russe de Monte Carlo. Black versus white was a pertinent issue for them as well. The tutus for these earlier productions, designed by Christian Bérard, were in contrasting black and white. The two duets were known as the black duet and the white duet.

How these apportionments of black and white affected the tone of the earlier ballets cannot be fully known, but suffice it to say that the emotional landscapes of many of Balanchine's ballets are hard to pin down. The subject is pressing for the last version, I think, because it was the last complete ballet Balanchine made. He made it for the New York City Ballet's Tchaikovsky Festival (June 10 to 14, 1981), and he died two years later. Given *Mozartiana*'s place in the history of his creative life, it is natural

Suzanne Farrell and children from the School of American Ballet in the opening "preghiera" of *Mozartiana*. New York City Ballet. Choreography by George
Balanchine © The George Balanchine Trust. Photo © by Costas.

to look retrospectively at the ballet and the festival itself to see signs of
impending tragedy.

Now, many years later, *Mozartiana* remains more black than white, but
to place it at death's doorstep, as some have done, seems extreme. The festival itself, however, was pretty morose. Its fatal flaw was that Balanchine
made few of the new works—perhaps because he was ailing at the time.
But there were other oddities that set the festival under cloudy skies.

Tchaikovsky's Mozartiana (the Suite No. 4) is so called because it is
the composer's homage to Mozart. The score begins with a gigue and is
followed by a minuet, the "preghiera" (or prayer), and a long theme and
variations in ten parts. Taking the liberty of moving the suite's third movement to the first, Balanchine chose to open the ballet with the preghiera
instead of the spritely gigue. In the preghiera the ballerina literally does

raise her arms in prayer, and the general soulfulness of the dance can't help but cast a sadness over the rest.

Balanchine's way of ending the festival was downright funereal. Setting the last movement, the "Adagio Lamentoso," of Tchaikovsky's sixth symphony, the "Pathétique" (written in 1893, the same year the composer died), he organized a pageant of angels and monks that ended with a young boy blowing out a candle, which plunged the stage into near darkness. Clearly, Balanchine had matters of life and death on his mind, but so had he in earlier ballets (such as *La Valse*, *Don Quixote*, and *Davidsbundlertanze*). The difference between the earlier ones and the Pathétique is that he died shortly after. So I, for one, resist looking into *Mozartiana* and the festival itself as if they were omens. Okay, so Balanchine was in a black mood in 1981, but to smell death when there is no corpse gives me the creeps.

Imagine, then, my discomfort when rereading a review I had written of *Mozartiana* the day after the premiere, for the *Soho Weekly News*. In her solos,

Farrell seems to be contemplating some kind of technical problem, some aspect of her weight. . . . On first viewing I can say only that her material has intellectual import. That her resolution of each statement—a flirtatious twist of her hips as she walks on pointe—has an ironic bravery that I find delightful and sad. And that the tone of her variations bespeaks the thing that can't be done. In the sense that *Mozartiana* seems to be about physical limitation, it seems to be about death. Now this may be way off the mark. After all, Farrell and Andersen get to do their pas de deux (though it isn't a love dance), and everyone celebrates at the end. . . . Yet in thinking about the way Farrell moves abruptly from pointe to flat foot, about the way she forces her leg to the back of her body instead of the front and about the way she prettily, delicately, charmingly investigates these maneuvers over and over again, and then in connecting these experiments with the prayer she offers at the beginning, I sense the ineffable sadness of human endeavor. The inwardness of her dancing suggests that neither the greatest ballerina nor choreographer of the day can transcend the body. Well, that's life, and *Mozartiana*, in raising the issue like no other ballet I have ever seen, is the chillier for it.

Today, *Mozartiana* seems less chilly than clinically observant, as if Balanchine had probed certain technical problems under a magnifying lens and then moved back from them to a dispassionate distance. *Mozartiana* is perhaps the opposite side of *Ballo della Regina*, created three years earlier for the virtuoso Merrill Ashley. In that piece, to Verdi music, he revels in all the complications he devises, and the effect is joyous. In the theme and variations section of the Tchaikovsky ballet, on the other hand, Balanchine and his ballerina ponder them, chew on them, won't let go of them until the composer forces them to by resolving each variation with three short notes followed by a witty plunk. The ballerina notes that plunk with a tap of the tip of her pointe shoe against the floor, or with a sudden fall to her flat foot. Then the music returns to another development of the theme, and the dancer starts out again on her errands into the maze—how the foot moves from back to front, and vice versa, how to cope with flat-footed turns and end up in fifth position, and so forth.

The subject of death rings out loud and clear in the earlier *Mozartianas*. That it reared its head—in my mind—in the 1981 version probably was because of the way Farrell danced it at the premiere. Ib Andersen, the male soloist in the theme and variations section, readily admitted to being unprepared on opening night, but it didn't show. Farrell was possibly in the process of digesting the material, and this might have been what gave her solos an effortful pressure, a sense of the thing that can't be done.

Today, it can be done; ballerinas all over the world do it all the time. It's still a knotty ballet though, but more about physical challenges than limitations. And contributing to that knottiness is the music, especially in the theme and variations. The music proceeds in fits and starts. Absent is the lyrical, seamless impetus characteristic of this composer. Balanchine could have imposed on the music his own steady movement forward,

Ib Andersen in the theme and variations section of *Mozartiana*. New York City Ballet. Choreography by George Balanchine © The George Balanchine Trust. Photo © by Costas.

but he chose to obey Tchaikovsky's pulse. As a result, *Mozartiana* is anti-romantic, almost cerebral.

The variations for the principal man are a different story, and you sense it from the first, as he suddenly breaks out into dazzling beats and turns. Although his choreography is incredibly tight-woven and intricate, much in the Bournonville style in which Andersen trained in Denmark, it is light and airy and it sings. How interesting that Balanchine assigned to the man the treble register of the music while handing over the bass to the woman. He plays Mozart to her Tchaikovsky. He—well, he just dances—while she pulls us into a miasma of tricky counts (like moving in five beats to the music's four). With each variation, the woman seems to be starting from day one. (Arlene Croce said her dances were like "a tape of herself run backward.") The man's solos, on the other hand, accumulate in power, reminiscent of the series of male/female variations in *Chaconne*. I'm not suggesting that his stuff is "better" than hers, but it certainly gives more overt pleasure; in terms of Balanchine's work for men, it is one of the most extraordinary essays in virtuosity. This is why I am disgruntled when people think of *Mozartiana* as Farrell's ballet. No, no, no—it's Andersen's too.

The theme and variations, about fifteen minutes long, is introduced by what Balanchine often called the "presentation" of the woman. That is, the couple simply walk about the stage, elaborating on the stroll with changes of direction and various exchanges of their arms. These slight complications of the promenade are one of my favorite Balanchinian devices, and they are no less delectable in *Mozartiana*. The first section of the pas de deux begins with the same idea, but is interrupted by a whirlwind visit from the four women of the minuet. The duet resumes with the ballerina extending her leg in a *grand développé à la seconde*, always a signal that the formal *grand pas de deux* is about to begin. Except that this pas de deux is neither formal nor grand nor even a proper duet, for it contains little supported movement. The two are always joining hands and separating, rendering their dance an extension of their solo variations. Again, the music's repeated opening statements and subsequent digressions—here highlighted by wild flights of the violin—interrupt the sustained rhythms we have come to expect from a pas de deux. The contemplative mood of the woman's earlier solos is felt in her walks on pointe as she circles around her partner. These walks were a Farrell specialty, so beautiful because of the way she lifted her extended leg ever so slightly just before placing it on the floor. But rather than color the mood with tenderness, intimacy, or poignancy, as they do in ballets like *Don Quixote* and *Diamonds*, her walks here convey inwardness, a feeling that she is thinking about something. Most pas de deux are for the audience; in *Mozartiana* we watch private moments.

The finale is cheerful, folksy, with all the dancers joining hands and galloping about in jigs reminiscent of the earlier gigue, danced by a lone man. But *Mozartiana* is obviously not a happy ballet; it's just that in Balanchine-land a finale is by definition upbeat, and so it is here. But why are the jigs charming in the finale and not in the gigue? Because, I think, the gigue has an intensity that borders on the fierce—its degree depending on the finesse of the dancer. It is fast, very fast, and rhythmically complex in its syncopations with music that is already syncopated. Most of all, it puts in extremis the *croisé* position, which even in its simplest shape is the most meaty position in the ballet vocabulary. In the gigue the man swings his front leg way, way across to the corner while his arms stretch as far as possible in the opposite direction. Then he repeats the phrase with his leg swinging behind his body, while his arms again counter the leg by moving in the opposite direction. Usually the *croisé* places a dancer in light and shadow; here, he moves so quickly and delicately that he seems to flicker between the two. Sometimes I wonder, who is this man, as if he were a character in a play. His first pose, all broken lines, recalls a harlequin or court jester. But the intensity of his solo precludes jocularity. Often he seems an interloper, breaking the spell of the preceding soulful preghiera. And sometimes the gigue character hints regret. The entrance of the minuet dancers overlaps with the gigue dancer's finish, and he remains on stage as the women begin their dance. He then walks off the stage slowly, twice looking back at them as they bow to him. He seems reluctant to leave. And depending on the dancer, his backward glances can convey a foreboding, or a secret, or what?

The mystery of the gigue man has never been resolved for me. There is another mystery in *Mozartiana* as well. After the duet couple conclude their introduction to the pas de deux, the four minuet women rush on and fly around the stage. The man and woman freeze, as if caught in a vision. We are all familiar with Siegfried's freeze when a vision of Odette appears during the festivities in the ballroom. Is there an unseen magician in *Mozartiana* putting the dancers out of commission, as von Rothbart does to Siegfried in *Swan Lake*? What is the meaning of the women's squall, or does it have no meaning other than as a response to the music's squall?

Mysterious goings-on are par for the course with Balanchine, and they are there in the earlier versions of *Mozartiana*, as well. From what I can glean from the Balanchine Foundation's videotape of reconstructed excerpts from the Ballet Russe version, there is one ultra-mysterious action, which was also in the first, 1933 version. It happens at the beginning of the preghiera, when a woman is suspended between two men dressed in black and is carried on stage as if in a funeral cortege. After she dances she is carried off, again suspended by her escorts. This is striking enough, but what grips the imagination most is the way she is carried: her suspended legs are just a few inches off the floor. Balanchine's corpse doesn't float prettily in the air; her proximity to the floor gives her an unsettling realism bordering on grotesquerie. How much effect this odd business had on the rest of the ballet is impossible to determine, yet several critics, Edwin Denby among them, spoke of the ballet's poignancy, ambiguousness, and perfume (qualities that Denby also ascribed to *Cotillon*, created a year earlier). Denby wrote that he didn't understand *Mozartiana*, but that of all the ballets he saw during the Ballets 1933 season, it was this one that most stuck in his head. I bet it's the image of the dead girl that visited Denby in his dreams.

The episode in which the minuet ladies storm around the stage prior to the pas de deux also has roots in the Ballet Russe's and possibly earlier versions, when a so-called gypsy woman tears about with her arms whipping through the air like crazy. Some photographs of earlier versions hint at other narrative undertones, showing the dancers' hands covering their eyes as if in mourning. And there is one shot of six women leaning over a man who lies absolutely prostrate on the floor. What in the devil is that image about? If these images reveal something basic about the emotional landscape of the earlier ballets, how does the scenery by Christian Bérard fit in? His backdrop depicted a sunny Italian square. Again, there's the question of how sunny and how dark, how white and how black the early *Mozartiana*s were.

Frederic Franklin, who is responsible for the partial reconstruction of the 1945 *Mozartiana* for the Balanchine Foundation, says in the video that the ballet he danced in was happier than the 1933 version he saw in London. He attributes the difference to the chic of Alexandra Danilova, the ballerina who was Franklin's partner in 1945, as compared to the youthful poignancy of Tamara Toumanova, a mere teenager in 1933. As for winning the grand sweepstakes for melancholy, I bet on the 1981 version—and not only because Rouben Ter-Arutunian outfitted the cast mostly in black. Certainly beginning it with the praying ballerina and her four guardian angels (young students) casts a shadow over all, including the spritely gigue character who may also be the outsider. The minuet has especially somber colorings. This very beautiful dance has large, expansive movements—high leg extensions and big jumps—but they are rendered grave by the music's slow tempo. Having to jump in adagio time accentuates the downward retreat of the jump rather than its upward thrust. How intriguing it is that Balanchine chose to devise steps that would normally require male partnering, that he boycotted the obvious.

One of the big questions about Balanchine's creative life is whether or not he got better as he got older. If you want to believe that chronological maturity brings artistic maturity—the most optimistic paradigm of creative life—then *Mozartiana* is your man. Comparing the 1945 ballet, even in its very truncated form as a reconstruction, with the later one, it's the later creation that wins hands down. It is by far the more sophisticated work. The earlier gigue, for example, it not as musically complex as the later; rather, it's a prototype of what came thirty-six years later. The ensemble dances (that is, what has been remembered) are pretty but elementary. And the two pas de deux in the 1945 version are conventional in form and steps; the 1981 edition is radical for the independence of the two dancers. There is, however, one absolutely gorgeous moment in the 1945 ballet. At the end of the duet the woman drapes herself across the man's knees as he pivots her in a descending circle so that her head finally rests on the floor, facing toward the audience. If this pose sounds familiar, it is. It's the same one that ends the adagio in *Symphony in C.* Balanchine lifted the pose from *Mozartiana*, never realizing, he said, that he would one day do another. So he had to come up with another conclusion to the duet.

The latest *Mozartiana* is a hard nut to crack. One admires it, to say the least, for its cerebral muscularity and for its technical craftsmanship at the very highest level. Yet the ballet doesn't sing to us, move us, and for this absence of lyrical force you must look to the music. I think that the Suite No. 4 simply doesn't have the *musique dansante* quality for which Balanchine loved Tchaikovsky. It's the music, not Balanchine's state of mind in 1981, that makes *Mozartiana* the ballet it is.

Suggested Reading

Ashley, Merrill. *Dancing for Balanchine*. New York: E. P. Dutton, 1985.

Balanchine, George. *Choreography by George Balanchine: A Catalogue of Works*. New York: Viking Penguin, 1984.

Balanchine, George, and Francis Mason. *Balanchine's Complete Stories of the Great Ballets*. Garden City, N.Y.: Doubleday, 1977.

Buckle, Richard, and John Taras. *George Balanchine: Ballet Master*. New York: Random House, 1988.

Costas. *Balanchine: Celebrating a Life in Dance*. Windsor, Conn.: Tide-Mark Press, 2003.

Duberman, Martin. *The Worlds of Lincoln Kirstein*. New York: Alfred A. Knopf, 2007.

Farrell, Suzanne. *Holding On to the Air*. Gainesville: University Press of Florida, 2002.

Fisher, Barbara Milberg. *In Balanchine's Company*. Middletown, Conn.: Wesleyan University Press, 2006

Garis, Robert. *Following Balanchine*. New Haven, Conn.: Yale University Press, 1995.

Goldner, Nancy. *The Stravinsky Festival of the New York City Ballet*. New York: Eakins Press, 1973.

———. *Balanchine Variations*. Gainesville: University Press of Florida, 2008.

Gottlieb, Robert. *George Balanchine: The Ballet Maker*. New York: HarperCollins, 2004.

———, ed. *Reading Dance*. New York: Pantheon, 2008.

Joseph, Charles M. *Stravinsky & Balanchine: A Journey of Invention*. New Haven, Conn.: Yale University Press, 2002.

Kent, Allegra. *Once a Dancer . . .* New York: St. Martins, 1997.

Kirstein, Lincoln. *Thirty Years of the New York City Ballet.* New York: Alfred A. Knopf, 1978.

Maiorano, Robert, and Valerie Brooks. *Balanchine's* Mozartiana. New York: Freundlich, 1985.

Martins, Peter. *Far from Denmark.* Boston: Little, Brown and Company, 1982.

Mason, Francis. *I Remember Balanchine.* New York: Doubleday, 1991.

Reynolds, Nancy. *Repertory in Review.* New York: Dial, 1997.

Schorer, Suki, and Russell Lee. *Suki Schorer on Balanchine Technique.* Gainesville: University Press of Florida, 2006.

Tallchief, Maria, and Larry Kaplan. *America's Prima Ballerina.* Gainesville: University Press of Florida, 2005.

Taper, Bernard. *Balanchine: A Biography.* New York: Times Books, 1984.

Villella, Edward, and Larry Kaplan. *Prodigal Son.* New York: Simon and Schuster, 1992.

Volkov, Solomon. *Balanchine's Tchaikovsky.* New York: Simon and Schuster, 1985.

Walczak, Barbara, and Una Kai. *Balanchine the Teacher.* Gainesville: University Press of Florida, 2008.